Microentrepreneurship in a Developing Country

Jagannadha Pawan Tamvada

Microentrepreneurship in a Developing Country

Evidence for Public Policy

palgrave
macmillan

Jagannadha Pawan Tamvada
University of Southampton
SOUTHAMPTON, UK

ISBN 978-3-030-68627-7 ISBN 978-3-030-68628-4 (eBook)
https://doi.org/10.1007/978-3-030-68628-4

This Palgrave Macmillan imprint is published by the registered company Springer Nature Switzerland AG.
The registered company address is: Gewerbestrasse 11, 6330 Cham, Switzerland

To the One who inspires all action

Acknowledgements

In summer 2004, I went to Germany to do my PhD with the late Stephan Klasen, a brilliant student of Amartya Sen and a stalwart at Goettingen who made seminal contributions to development economics research in Germany. That summer, I proposed to David Audretsch at the Max Planck Institute of Economics that understanding entrepreneurship in developing countries can open new avenues for their economic prosperity. David Audretsch, the champion of small business and entrepreneurship for economic growth, gave me a three-year fellowship to study entrepreneurship in the context of my home country—India. Thus began my journey at the confluence of these two giants' intellectual traditions, to whom I am truly indebted.

Many individuals and organisations supported my work over the years that followed. I am grateful to them for all their support. The most recent addition to this long list is the newly formed India Centre at the University of Southampton that has supported my work and embraced the iPowerz initiative that fast-tracks microentrepreneurship and small business growth.

At every stage, Liz Barlow at Palgrave Macmillan has shared helpful insights in producing this book, and Charanya Manoharan has generously offered her time. I thank them for all their patience and support.

Portions of Chap. 2 have been published as Tamvada (2010) and portions of Chap. 3 as Tamvada (2015). Portions of Chap. 4 are based on work that I co-authored with David Audretsch and Chap. 5 is based on material published in Coad and Tamvada (2012). I thank the publishers of *Small Business Economics* for permission to publish material from Entrepreneurship and Welfare (2010, 34, 65–79) and Firm Growth and Barriers to Growth Among Small Firms in India by Coad and Tamvada (39, 383–400). My thanks also go to the publishers of *Regional Studies* for permission to publish from The Spatial Distribution of Self-employment in India: Evidence from Geoadditive Models (2015, 49, 300–322).

I remain eternally grateful to my guru Bhagwan Sri Sathya Sai Baba for shaping every moment of this journey with unconditional love. I thank my family for their love and affection.

Contents

List of Figures

List of Tables

1

Microentrepreneurship: An Interdisciplinary View

More than 50 years ago, Baumol (1968, p. 71) proclaimed, "in a growth conscious world I remain convinced that encouragement of the entrepreneur is the key to the stimulation of growth." In recent years, the economics of entrepreneurship emerged as a compelling subject, and a vast literature has emerged providing insights into the many facets of entrepreneurship. Though each such facet is incomplete by itself, together they offer a comprehensive understanding of entrepreneurial choice, new firm formation and the role of entrepreneurship in economic growth.

Reflecting a broad consensus that has emerged over time, Lazear (2005, p. 1) suggested, "the entrepreneur is the single most important player in the economy." Indeed, it is so. However, entrepreneurship mostly occurs in micro forms with less than 1% of firms having more than 10 employees even in developed countries. While some micro entrepreneurs are solo self-employed, others have employees and are organized as small firms. While some are registered, a large number of them are unregistered own account workers. This book sheds light on microentrepreneurship in one eminent context—India. It examines microentrepreneurship from multiple angles—in the form of self-employed individuals, employer

J. P. Tamvada, *Microentrepreneurship in a Developing Country*,
https://doi.org/10.1007/978-3-030-68628-4_1

entrepreneurs, new firm start-ups, and micro and small firms using the lens of economic geography to offer a comprehensive picture of microentrepreneurship in a developing country, its distribution across space, the role of individual and spatial characteristics in shaping occupational choice and the size of new firms, the economic returns to microentrepreneurship and the challenges facing microentrepreneurs.

A significant proportion of entrepreneurial activity in a developing country setting is usually in the informal sector that consists of self-employed individuals, unregistered enterprises, and small businesses. While distinct academic disciplines such as labour economics, industrial economics and, more recently, entrepreneurship research in business and management studies, examine these, this book brings them together for an interdisciplinary empirical assessment. For this, we examine the nexus between the entrepreneur, the firm, and the region for drawing a comprehensive picture of how the spatial location simultaneously determines the occupational choice at an individual level and the size of new firms emerging in a region using large-scale databases of individuals and firms from India. In the process, the book offers some fresh insights for shaping public policy in developing countries that aim to pursue entrepreneurship led growth.

Historically, an impression of noncompetitive labour markets in less developed countries (LDCs) rendered their entrepreneurial sectors uninteresting to scholars researching the personality of entrepreneurs. Harris and Todaro (1970), for instance, predicted that absence of economic opportunities, combined with high unemployment, forces individuals into low productivity self-employment. There is growing evidence, however, that the labour markets of developing countries are actually competitive, and that entrepreneurship is not merely a subsistence level activity there. Whilst revisiting these theories, Chap. 2 provides a broad overview of the role of spatial location in shaping the nature of self-employment using large-scale databases from India. It analyses the role of geographic location as a micro-determinant of self-employment choice while examining the impact of human capital accumulation on occupational choice in agricultural and nonagricultural sectors in India.

Further shedding light on the nature of self-employment in the Indian context, Chap. 3 examines the returns to occupational choice using the per-capita consumption expenditure to circumvent the problem arising from income underreporting by self-employed individuals. This analysis, using quantile regressions, reveals the existence of a welfare hierarchy in occupations across the welfare distribution wherein entrepreneurs employing others have the highest returns in terms of consumption, while entrepreneurs working for themselves, that is, the self-employed individuals, have slightly lower returns than the salaried employees do. However, self-employment entails higher returns than casual labour and a relative escape from poverty.

Turning attention to small firms, Chap. 4 examines the role of geographic location as a micro-determinant of firm start-up size. Here, we find that the size of new firm start-ups exhibits remarkable spatial patterns even after controlling for the firm and industry characteristics. The results reveal a clear north-south divide in the size of new firm start-ups in India. An investigation into the factors that shape these residual spatial patterns shows that regions that are more developed give birth to superior start-ups. Glaringly, these spatial patterns have an inverse relationship with the spatial patterns of self-employment presented in Chap. 2 suggesting that start-ups experience a size penalty in regions where individuals are more likely to be self-employed. These results have significant implications for public policy related to entrepreneurship led economic development that many developing countries are beginning to adopt and underscore the need to rethink such a development policy.

For a more complete analysis of microentrepreneurship, Chap. 5 looks beyond start-ups to enter the arena of small businesses. It investigates the factors shaping their growth and decline using a fairly representative large-scale database of small businesses in India. The chapter suggests that size and age have a negative impact on firm growth and enterprises managed by women have lower expected growth rates. Furthermore, proprietary firms face lower growth on the whole, especially if they are young firms, and exporting has a positive effect on firm growth, especially for young firms and for female-owned firms. Only some small firms are able to convert know-how into commercial success, while many others are unable to translate it into superior growth.

In Chap. 6, the insights from the preceding chapters are consolidated to develop a new model reflecting the relationship between microentrepreneurship and economic development. This chapter links occupational choice of individuals and entrant firms' start-up size in the spatial context that simultaneously determines the two processes. This link is established using a simple model of occupational choice, firm start-up size and the spatial location that relates the dynamics of micro-entrepreneurship to the process of economic development. The resulting public policy implications are discussed to provide a roadmap for entrepreneurship led economic development.

A government eager to support entrepreneurship for economic development is likely to focus on creating new start-ups. However, there is a need to look more closely the 99% of enterprise activity taking shape in the form of microentrepreneurship in a developing country context. This book sets out to examine the multiple facets of microentreprenurship in India, particularly in the forms of self-employment as well as start-ups and small businesses, with an aim to draw policy implications.

To sum up the core results, we find that regions that are poorest are more likely to have the greatest numbers of self-employed individuals. New firm start-ups in such regions tend to experience a size penalty. They are of smaller size than new firm start-ups in regions that are more developed. Furthermore, a hierarchy in returns to occupations across the welfare distributions suggests that self-employed individuals are sandwiched between salaried employees and casual labourers when it comes to their economic returns. Thus, although self-employed individuals have lower returns than salaried employees, they do much better than individuals who work as casual labourers. For this reason, transitioning into self-employment is a step up for individuals who may otherwise become labourers. On similar lines, employers have greater returns than salaried employees. Thus, individuals transitioning from salaried employment into entrepreneurial activities that create jobs are likely to experience higher returns. A policy environment that supports such transitions enables welfare gains while economic, social, and cultural barriers that inhibit such transitions lead to net welfare losses.

In addition to focusing on creating new start-ups, it is essential to create an environment that enables start-ups with larger size to emerge while offering existing small firms accelerated growth opportunities. Interventions through public investments to drive economic and financial development of regions such as, for example, those that facilitate large-scale industrialisation, can subsequently give birth to new firms that have a larger size at start-up. Furthermore, a uniform entrepreneurship policy across different regions, as in the case of a policy decided at national level, may ignore subtle aspects of microentrepreneurship taking shape at regional levels and lead to sub-optimal outcomes if it does not improve the conditions that influence the growth of firms.

References

Baumol, W. J. (1968). Entrepreneurship in economic theory. *The American Economic Review, 58* (2), Papers and Proceedings of the Eightieth Annual Meeting of the American Economic Association, 64–71.

Harris, J. R., & Todaro, M. P. (1970). Migration, unemployment and development: A two sector analysis. *American Economic Review, 60*(1), 126–142.

Lazear, E. (2005). Entrepreneurship. *Journal of Labour Economics, 23*(4), 649–680.

2

The Spatial Distribution of Self-Employment

There are two competing theories of labour markets in developing countries—the disadvantage theory and the comparative advantage theory. The disadvantage theory hypothesizes that people who are rationed out of the formal labour market are compelled to take up self-employment or take employment as workers in household enterprises. Such people are considered to constitute the *informal sector*. Thus, beginning with the labour surplus model of Lewis (1954), the labour markets of developing countries are viewed as dualistic markets segmented along the formal-informal lines (also see Sen, 1966; Ranis & Fei, 1961; Harris & Todaro, 1970).[1] However, proponents of the comparative advantage theory find evidence against this idea of low-level subsistence self-employment in LDCs (Blau, 1986; Chiswick, 1976; Majumdar, 1981; Mohapatra,

[1] Lewis (1954) argued that if wage rate is determined competitively in the rural areas of a LDC then it will be below the subsistence levels. Harris and Todaro (1970) predicted that workers who migrate from rural to urban areas face unemployment and are forced to work in household enterprises at subsistence levels. Models of rural-urban migration following this line of thought hypothesize that the urban informal sector acts as a refuge for migrants and excess labour in urban areas are forced to take up low productivity self-employment.

J. P. Tamvada, *Microentrepreneurship in a Developing Country*,
https://doi.org/10.1007/978-3-030-68628-4_2

Rozelle, & Goodhue, 2007; Rosenzweig, 1980) hypothesizing, instead, that individuals choose employment in the so-called informal sector when competitive opportunities are perceived (Gindling, 1991; Magnac, 1991; Maloney, 2004).[2] Maloney (2004, p. 1159) notes that "as a first approximation we should think of the informal sector as the unregulated, developing country analogue of the voluntary entrepreneurial small firm sector found in advanced countries, rather than a residual comprised of disadvantaged workers rationed out of good jobs." In this chapter, we examine if variations in self-employment across regions can shed fresh light on the nature of self-employment in a developing country.

2.1 Spatial Location and Self-employment

Both individuals' personal characteristics (Evans & Leighton, 1989b; Kihlstrom & Laffont, 1979) and regional factors (Georgellis & Wall, 2000) influence entrepreneurial decisions, and entrepreneurial activity occurs with persistent regional variations (Georgellis & Wall, 2000; Robson, 1998). Parker (2005) models variations in entrepreneurship rates across regions as self-perpetuating and self-reinforcing occupational structures that result in multiple entrepreneurship equilibria leading to a conjecture that individuals in neighbouring regions may exhibit similar occupational preferences because the presence of many self-employed people in a neighbourhood may induce others to choose self-employment voluntarily or because of the absence of alternative options.

There are three standard approaches to analysing the role of region in self-employment choice. The first approach controls for the influence of the region through dummy variables (Blanchflower & Oswald, 1998;

[2] More recently, a growing body of literature attempts to capture the heterogeneity within the informal sector. This strand of literature argues that the informal sector is a blend of both disadvantaged and competitive sectors (Cunningham & Maloney, 2001; Fields, 2005; Guenther & Launov, 2006) and claims simultaneous presence of disadvantaged "lower" and voluntary "upper" tiers within the informal sector. Pratap and Quintin (2006) do not find any evidence for segmented labour markets in Argentina. Yamada (1996) finds evidence of voluntary self-selection and higher earnings in self-employment in informal sector in Peru.

Borjas & Bronars, 1989; Fairlie & Meyer, 1996; Robson, 1998). Here a large number of dummy variables are introduced into the estimation for examining the impact of spatial location at a micro level. The second approach simultaneously estimates individual as well as regional characteristics as factors shaping self-employment choice (Blanchflower & Oswald, 1998; Evans & Jovanovic, 1989; Glaeser, 2007). The third approach analyses determinants of region-level self-employment figures, based on aggregated data, and estimates the quantity of entrepreneurial activity as a function of regional variables such as unemployment and tax rates (Foelster, 2002; Georgellis & Wall, 2000; Torrini, 2005). These techniques, however, do not allow estimation of spatial location as a continuous variate that can shed light on the dependence of the self-employment choice on neighbouring regions, and do not focus on estimating spatial self-employment patterns that remain after controlling for individual characteristics.

Using geoadditive models to overcome some of these limitations allows incorporation of spatial location as a micro determinant of self-employment choice. Here, the impact of spatial location on self-employment choice is modelled as a continuous variate. This enables visualization of these self-employment neighbourhoods, and the estimated spatial patterns reflect the propensity of people to be self-employed in a region after controlling for other individual-level effects allowing *ceteris paribus* interpretation.

2.2 Individual Determinants of Self-employment

Broadly there is consensus that age, gender, education, marital status, wealth, and social class influence self-employment choice along with spatial location.[3] For example, most empirical evidence suggests a positive relationship between age and entrepreneurship (Blanchflower, 2000; Blanchflower & Meyer, 1994; Evans & Leighton, 1989a). The probability of being self-employed increases with age as it is only over time that individuals accumulate more of the human capital and resources needed

[3] Parker (2018) extensively reviews the individual specific characteristics that shape occupational choice. For brevity these are not discussed here extensively.

for starting a new venture,[4] although some theoretical studies claim that younger workers choose entrepreneurship and they are more likely to engage in riskier projects (Johnson, 1978; Jovanovic, 1979; Miller, 1984). Similarly, married individuals are more likely to be self-employed than their unmarried counterparts as they can jointly raise a greater amount of capital for the start-up, and the risk inherent in self-employment is reduced if the entrepreneur's spouse is employed elsewhere or otherwise (Blanchflower & Oswald, 1998; Borjas, 1986). For these reasons, age and marital status are likely to have a positive impact on the probability of being self-employed.

The role of education in the entrepreneurial decision is much less clear. On the one hand, education increases managerial ability and expected entrepreneurial performance, which can lead to a higher probability of entrepreneurship (Calvo & Wellisz, 1980; Lucas, 1978; Van Praag & Cramer, 2001). On the other hand, it increases the returns to wage employment and may disincentivize self-employment choice (Iyigun & Owen, 1999). Thus, there is no consensus in the literature on the effect of education on self-employment (Van der Sluis, Van Praag, & Vijverberg, 2005) as it expands an individual's knowledge base and increases exposure to new opportunities whilst also increasing the opportunity cost of being self-employed. Under the assumption that entrepreneurship is riskier than providing professional services, Iyigun and Owen (1999) show that as an economy develops, individuals begin to invest more time in accumulating professional skills by way of education than in accumulating entrepreneurial human capital. This suggests that returns to salaried employment increase faster than returns to entrepreneurship as per-capita income grows, with the result being that individuals have more to lose by engaging in entrepreneurship (Lucas, 1978). Thus, individuals who are more educated are likely to opt for salaried employment in a developing country context.

Another determinant of self-employment is wealth. Wealthier individuals have more of a "safety net" when embarking on a new venture than their less wealthy counterparts do. As Bohacek (2006, p. 2196) notes, "In order not to default on loan contracts, entrepreneurs can

[4] Goedhuys and Sleuwaegen (2000), for instance, find this to be true for individuals in Cote d'Ivoire.

borrow only limited amounts secured by collateral. This collateral (accumulated assets) guarantees not only the repayment of the loan but also positive consumption of the entrepreneur in the case of a project's failure. As the financial constraint is endogenously related to a borrower's wealth, entrepreneurship becomes positively correlated with wealth." Households with very high levels of wealth have a higher propensity to take risk (Carroll, 2000) and are most likely to be business owners (Hurst & Lusardi, 2004). Similarly, Blanchflower and Oswald (1998) find that inheritance increases the probability of self-employment, and Banerjee and Neuman (1993) suggest that wealth distribution determines the occupational structure in an economy. In the Indian context, Audretsch et al. (2013) suggest that socio-cultural backgrounds have an effect on occupational choice. The effects of these variables have to be filtered out to estimate the impact of spatial location on self-employment. This is achieved using geoadditive models as discussed in the following sections.

2.3 Self-employment Across Space in India

The data used for the analysis are derived from the 60th-round employment-unemployment survey of the NSSO of India, conducted in 2004.[5] As the focus is on economically active individuals, the sample is restricted to those who are older than 15 but younger than 70 years of age. This reduces the sample size from 303,811 to 204,298. The principal economic activity of this sample ranges from domestic duties to full-time employment (in the form of salaried employment, self-employment, casual labour, or unemployment).

Table 2.1 lists the number of individuals in different occupational categories. Individuals who are unpaid family workers, students, domestic workers, pensioners, those who are unable to work due to disabilities, and people who reported belonging to the occupational class 'other' are dropped from the database. This reduces the final sample to 88,623

[5] The NSSO is an Indian government organization that collects regular socio-economic data in India from households and enterprises. It conducts large-scale sample surveys for the government of India. It was set-up in the year 1950. The NSSO is responsible for survey design and implementation. The surveyors are sent with a standardised survey questionnaire to collect household data from different regions of India.

Table 2.1 Distribution of occupation

	Total number	Percentage	Cumulative
Self-employed (own account workers)	37,197	18.21	18.21
Self-employed (employers)	922	0.45	18.66
Household helpers (unpaid family worker)	23,505	11.51	30.16
Salaried employees	21,223	10.39	40.55
Casual labour (public)	310	0.15	40.70
Casual labour (other)	23,823	11.66	52.36
Unemployed	5,148	2.52	54.88
Students	25,853	12.65	67.54
Only domestic duties	40,894	20.02	87.56
Domestic duties and collection of wood etc.	18,045	8.83	96.39
Pensioners	2,645	1.29	97.68
Not working due to disability	1,381	0.68	98.36
Others	3352	1.65	100
Total	204,298	100	

individuals. Thus only those who reported their primary occupation as self-employed (includes own account workers and employers), salaried employees, casual labourers, or unemployed are included in the final database.[6] Due to missing values of some of the variables, the estimations use only 86,140 data points.

The descriptive statistics in Table 2.2 show that 65% of the individuals have attended at least primary school, 65% live in rural areas, and 40% are employed in the agricultural sector. More than 50% of individuals in agriculture are self-employed in comparison to a relatively lower proportion of self-employed in the nonagriculture sector.

2.3.1 Geoadditive Model of Self-employment Choice

The methodological details of the Bayesian semiparametric geoadditive models used for the estimations are presented in Appendix 1. This methodology is widely used in the spatial statistics literature (Fahrmeir &

[6] Dropping the unemployed does not fundamentally alter the main results of this chapter. Individuals in the island states of Daman and Diu, Dadra and Nagar Haveli, Andaman and Nicobar Islands, and Lakshadweep are excluded from the database as the geoadditive models cannot be estimated when continuity in space does not exist.

Table 2.2 Agricultural and nonagricultural sectors (descriptives)

Variable	All	Non-Agri	Agri
Self-employed	0.430	0.341	0.564
Age	37.130	34.910	40.464
Age (Std. Dev)	12.88	12.08	13.31
Male	0.809	0.837	0.767
Female	0.191	0.163	0.233
Unmarried	0.210	0.278	0.108
Married	0.745	0.690	0.828
Divorced	0.045	0.032	0.064
No education	0.256	0.135	0.437
Informal education	0.085	0.066	0.115
Primary school	0.310	0.319	0.298
High school	0.227	0.294	0.126
University	0.122	0.186	0.024
No technical education	0.948	0.919	0.991
Technical degree	0.009	0.014	0.001
Technical diploma	0.043	0.067	0.007
Rural	0.649	0.453	0.943
Urban	0.351	0.547	0.057
Agriculture	0.400	0.000	1.000
Land < 0.2 hectares	0.214	0.295	0.093
0.2 < land < 0.4 hectares	0.461	0.526	0.362
0.4 < land < 2 hectares	0.241	0.137	0.396
Land > 2 hectares	0.084	0.041	0.149
Hindu	0.792	0.777	0.815
Backward	0.676	0.612	0.772
N	88623	53202	35421

Kneib, 2011, as surveyed in) that has emerged parallel to the pioneering work in spatial econometrics (Anselin, 1988; Lesage & Pace, 2009). Although both these strands of scholarship aim at estimating the role of space, they have adopted different approaches to modelling spatial location. The methods in the spatial statistics literature (Fahrmeir & Kneib, 2011) are formulated as latent spatial models where spatial location is part of the linear predictor of a spatial regression model; in contrast, the direct spatial autoregressive models (Lesage & Pace, 2009) presume spatial structures for the response variables. Comparing these two forms of spatial estimations, (Fahrmeir & Kneib, 2011, pp. 344–346) note that one of the greatest advantages of the latent models is their applicability to general types of responses like ordered categorical responses or survival times and in cases where it is difficult to estimate using the direct approach. Furthermore, the methodology allows researchers to simultaneously estimate impact of spatial location along with the non-linear effects of continuous covariates like age, and covariates that are not continuous. These developments in spatial statistics offer a new opportunity to model space in many non-linear, discrete, and longitudinal settings.

Using the Bayesian geoadditive methodology, individual characteristics as well as spatial location are introduced simultaneously in the following generalized semi-parametric geoadditive regression framework.

$$H = \gamma_{\text{const}} + \gamma_{\text{individual\_characteristics}} + f_{\text{age}} + f_{\text{spatial}}(\text{district}) + f_{\text{random}}(\text{district})$$

The *dependent variable* is occupational status of an individual and takes value 1 if self-employed and 0 otherwise. Three geoadditive models are estimated for different subsamples of the database. The first geoadditive model is estimated on the entire sample. The second geoadditive model is estimated for a subsample of individuals in nonagriculture. The third geoadditive model is estimated for a subsample of individuals working in agriculture.

The estimation output for each model comprises of a table with estimated effects of the parametric part of the above equation, non-linear effects of age, and four maps with the estimated spatial effects. The spatial maps are presented as follows. In the sub-plot (a) of the maps, the estimated posterior mean of the structured spatial effects are given. As the methodology described in Appendix 1 shows, the structured spatial effects model spatial dependence and estimate the impact of space as a continuous variate. A green colour in the legend below the map indicates that a region has a positive impact on the likelihood of individuals choosing self-employment, and a red colour indicates that the region has a negative impact on choosing self-employment. In the sub-plot (c), the map shows if the estimated spatial effects in sub-plot (a) are statistically significant at 95% confidence level, and in sub-plot (d) the map shows if the estimated spatial effects in sub-plot (a) are statistically significant at 80% confidence level. A white colour in these plots indicates that the impact of the spatial unit on self-employment is significantly positive, and a black colour indicates that the impact is significantly negative. The sub-plot (b) gives the estimated results for the localized random effects—unlike the structured spatial effects given in (a), these effects are estimated at the local district level. These effects correspond to the random error component of the above models.

The dependent variable is occupational status of an individual and takes value 1 if the individual is self-employed and 0 otherwise. The Bayesian software package BayesX is used for the estimations.[7]

$$\eta = \gamma_{\text{const}} + \gamma_{\text{female}} + \gamma_{\text{marital\_status}} + \gamma_{\text{education\_general}} + \gamma_{\text{education\_technical}} + \gamma_{\text{wealth}} + \gamma_{\text{urban}} + \gamma_{\text{agri}} + \gamma_{\text{hindu}} + \gamma_{\text{backward}} + f_{\text{age}} + f_{\text{spatial}}(\text{district}) + f_{\text{random}}(\text{district})$$

The results of the parametric part of this regression model, shown in Table 2.3, suggest that both married and divorced people are more likely to be self-employed compared to unmarried individuals.[8] The positive coefficients of the education variables of informal and school education suggest that lower levels of education are positively related to self-employment. The negative coefficient of the variable 'university' suggests that higher education decreases the probability of self-employment. The effect of having a technical degree is insignificant and having a technical diploma is negative and significant at the 5% level. The probability of being self-employed also increases with the wealth of the individual's household, which is proxied here using the amount of land owned by a household.[9] However, this result should be interpreted

[7] The nonlinear effect of age is modelled as third-degree P-splines with a second-order random walk penalty with the number of equidistant knots assumed to be 20. The structured spatial effects are estimated based on Markov random field priors and random spatial effects are estimated with Gaussian priors. The variance component in all the cases are estimated based on inverse gamma priors with hyperparameters a = 0.001 and b = 0.001. The number of iterations is set to 110000 with burnin parameter set to 10000 and the thinning parameter set to 100. The autocorrelation files and the sampling paths show that the MCMC algorithm has converged. These plots are available from the author.

[8] This is consistent with Taylor (1996), Fairlie and Meyer (1996) and other studies that find positive effects of marital status on self-employment.

[9] The problem of endogeneity with respect to land even in the agricultural sector may not be so severe, as only those who possess land may be able to choose self-employment. The database has some information on the purchases made on the some durable commodities for some households. However, the information is missing for a number of households and for a number of items in the representative consumption bundle. Furthermore, as income data is not available for the majority of individuals in the sample, the land possessed cannot be instrumented using income data.

Table 2.3 Determinants of self-employment (*Geoadditive model 1*)

Variable	Mean	Std. Dev.	2.5%-Qt.	97.5%-Qt.
Personal characteristics				
Female	−0.398	0.014	−0.426	−0.372
Married	0.175	0.018	0.141	0.211
Divorced	0.317	0.029	0.259	0.376
General education				
Informal	0.265	0.019	0.227	0.304
Primary school	0.332	0.014	0.304	0.360
High school	0.193	0.016	0.163	0.224
University	−0.181	0.020	−0.218	−0.141
Technical education				
Technical degree	−0.127	0.057	−0.232	0.016
Technical diploma	−0.117	0.026	−0.168	−0.068
Land possessed				
0.2 < land < 0.4 hectares	0.149	0.014	0.120	0.176
0.4 < land < 2 hectares	0.791	0.017	0.758	0.824
Land > 2 hectares	1.180	0.024	1.132	1.226
Location				
Urban	0.253	0.013	0.227	0.279
Agriculture	0.336	0.013	0.312	0.361
Religion & Social Group				
Hindu	−0.205	0.014	−0.233	−0.179
Backward	−0.183	0.012	−0.206	−0.160
Constant	−0.545	0.027	−0.599	−0.492
N	86140			
Deviance (Mean)	93422.587			
Std. Dev.	36.196992			
Deviance (μ)	92973.92			
pD	448.66642			
DIC	93871.253			

Notes: Dependent variable is binary self-employment status of the individual. Base categories for marital status, general education, technical education, land dummies are unmarried, no general education, no technical education and less than 0.2 hectares of land respectively. The confidence interval is given in the last two columns

with some caution, as land is potentially endogenous with respect to occupation.[10] Nevertheless, the land variables are retained, as there are compelling reasons to assume that wealth determines entrepreneurial

[10] In the absence of a good instruments for wealth, probit models are estimated with and without the land variables to check if the land variable adversely affects the coefficients of the other variables and find no evidence of such effects. A Hausman test to test for changes in coefficients of other variables shows that the results are consistent.

choice.[11] The results also suggest that Hindus and members of backward castes are less likely to be self-employed.

Figure 2.1a shows that the probability of being self-employed increases with age, confirming the age effect. The derivative of the 'age' function in Fig. 2.1b indicates that the marginal effect of age on self-employment choice first increases, then drops, and then increases again very rapidly for individuals older than 55 years. The rise in the 50s is consistent with the findings of empirical literature on developed countries (Blanchflower, 2000; Blanchflower & Meyer, 1994) that older individuals are more likely to be self-employed.[12] As Fuchs (1982, p. 356) claims: "Men who change to self-employment late in life are primarily those who have had previous experience in self-employment or who are in wage-and-salary occupations such as managers or salesmen that have many characteristics similar to self-employment." The self-employed often continue to work even after the retirement age at which salaried employees stop working. Switches to self-employment may reflect a partial-retirement effect, as salaried workers switch to self-employment instead of dropping out of the labour force toward the end of the life course (Quinn, 1980). This leads to oversampling of older self-employed, and could explain the increase at 55 years.

The map of structured spatial effects in Fig. 2.2a shows the presence of strong spatial effects and a clear north-south divide in the probability of self-employment, a finding confirmed by Figs. 2.2c and d, which plot the 95% and 80% confidence intervals for the estimated structured spatial effect and show the presence of neighbourhood effects that spill over district as well as state boundaries. These spatial patterns are residual spatial patterns and allow *ceteris paribus* interpretation, as the individual factors that influence self-employment choice, such as age, gender, and education, are controlled for in the geoadditive framework. People in the northern states of Uttar Pradesh and Bihar have a higher likelihood of being self-employed than those residing in southern regions. The local unstructured random effects in Fig. 2.2b are very small as compared to

[11] One of the primary reasons for keeping these indicators of household wealth is that there is evidence of the financial institutions rationing credit to individuals who are able to provide collateral. This indicates that wealth should strongly predict the self-employment choice as lack of finance is one of the biggest obstacles to being self-employed.

[12] Retirements effects are also associated with this phenomena.

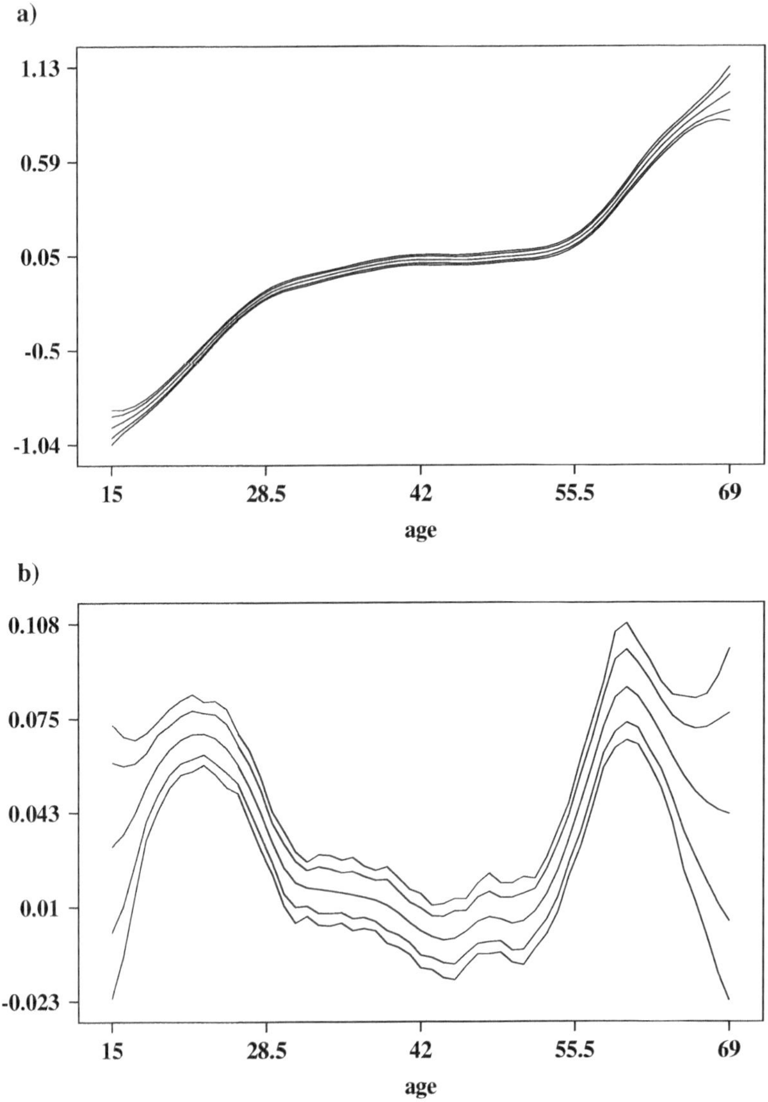

Fig. 2.1 Non-linear effect of age on self-employment (*Geoadditive model 1*). (a) Posterior mean of the non-linear effect of 'age' together with 95% and 80% point-wise credible intervals in Geoadditive model 1. (b) Derivative of the posterior mean of the 'age' function with 95% and 80% point-wise credible intervals in Geoadditive model 1

(a)

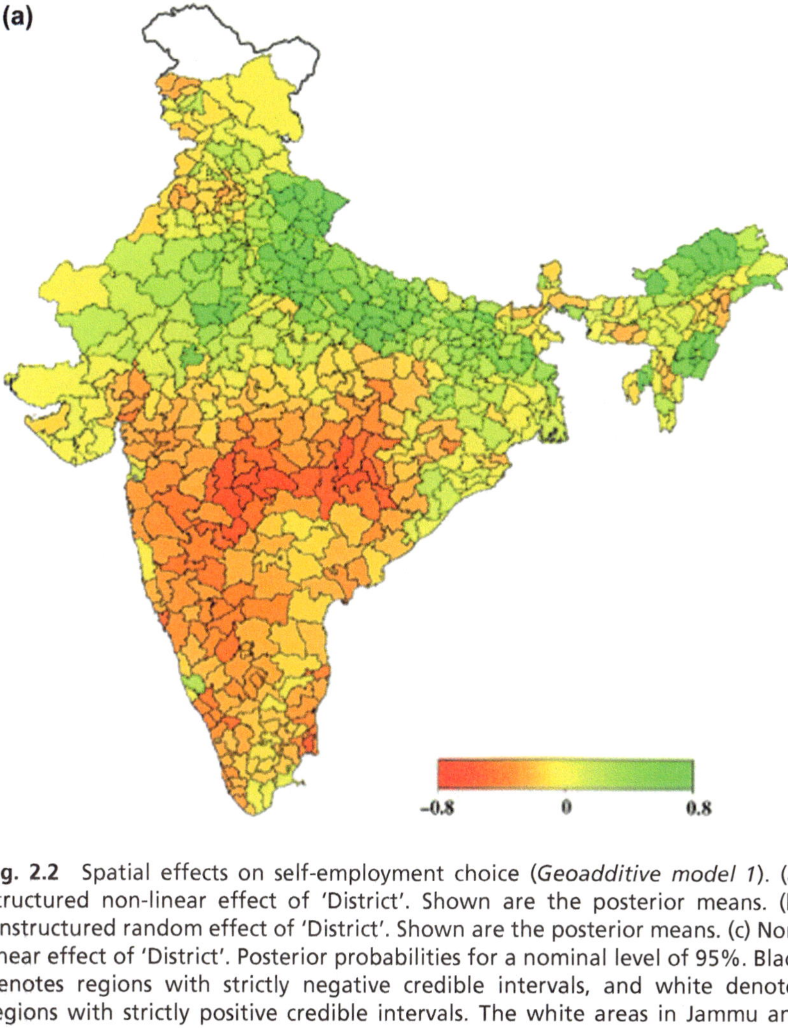

Fig. 2.2 Spatial effects on self-employment choice (*Geoadditive model 1*). (a) Structured non-linear effect of 'District'. Shown are the posterior means. (b) Unstructured random effect of 'District'. Shown are the posterior means. (c) Non-linear effect of 'District'. Posterior probabilities for a nominal level of 95%. Black denotes regions with strictly negative credible intervals, and white denotes regions with strictly positive credible intervals. The white areas in Jammu and Kashmir are regions not included in the estimations. (d) Non-linear effect of 'District'. Posterior probabilities for a nominal level of 80%. Black denotes regions with strictly negative credible intervals, and white denotes regions with strictly positive credible intervals. The white areas in Jammu and Kashmir are regions not included in the estimations

(b)

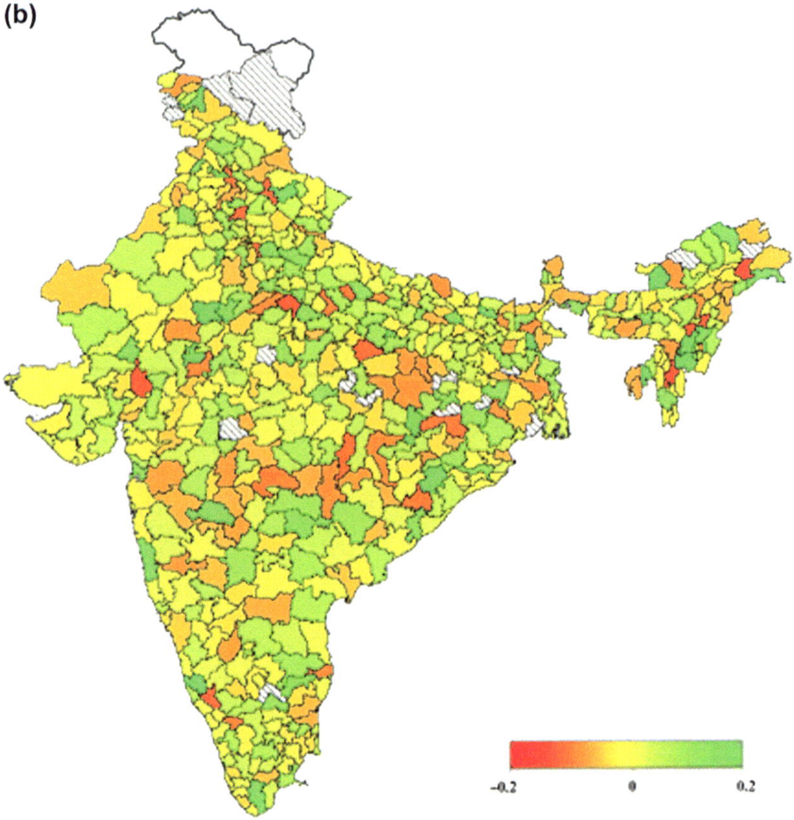

Fig. 2.2 (continued)

(c)

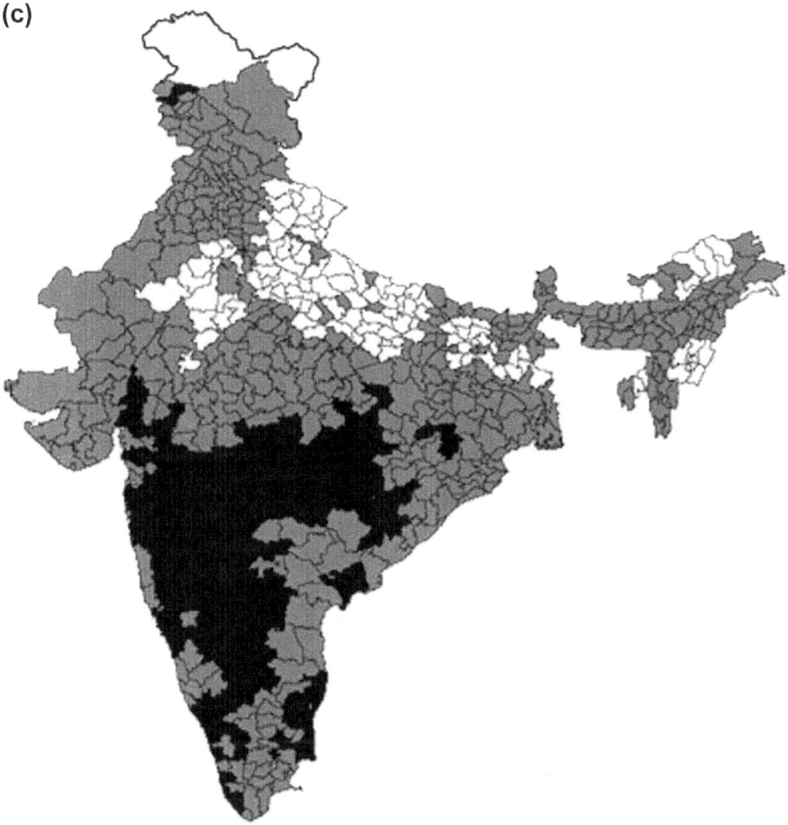

Fig. 2.2 (continued)

(d)

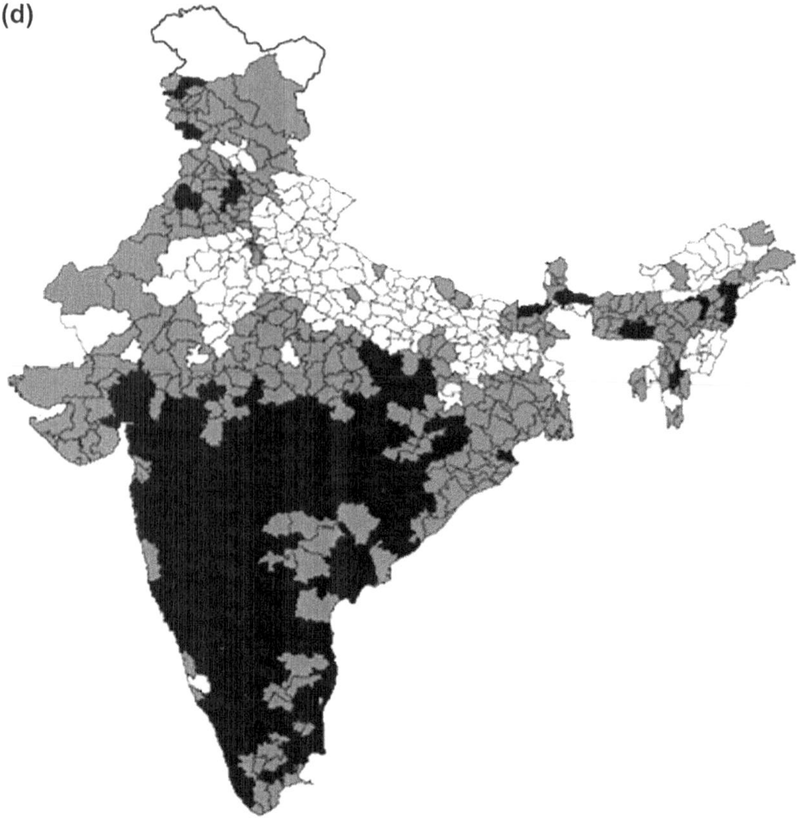

Fig. 2.2 (continued)

the structured effects, and indicate that impact of spatial location is continuous and not random.[13] To shed more light on these spatial patterns, sector-specific models are estimated in the next subsection.

2.3.2 Geoadditive Models of Agricultural and Nonagricultural Self-Employment

The first model assumes that the determinants of self-employment are the same for all self-employed individuals in agricultural as well as in nonagriculture. To examine the differences in the two sectors, the following semiparametric model is estimated separately for individuals in agricultural and nonagricultural sectors:[14]

$$\eta = \gamma_{\text{const}} + \gamma_{\text{female}} + \gamma_{\text{marital\_status}} + \gamma_{\text{education\_general}} + \gamma_{\text{education\_technical}} + \gamma_{\text{wealth}} + \gamma_{\text{urban}} + \gamma_{\text{hindu}} + \gamma_{\text{backward}} + \mathrm{f}_{\text{age}} + \mathrm{f}_{\text{spatial}}(\text{district}) + \mathrm{f}_{\text{random}}(\text{district})$$

Tables 2.4 and 2.5 show considerable differences in the relative human capital endowments of self-employed individuals in the two sectors. In the agricultural sector, those with higher levels of human capital (measured by age and education) are more likely to be self-employed, whereas in the nonagricultural sector, such individuals are more likely to be salaried employees. Belonging to a lower social class is significantly negatively related to being self-employed in both sectors; being a Hindu has a significant negative relationship in nonagriculture only.

In the nonagricultural sector, as Fig. 2.3a shows, the age function increases at a decreasing rate until age 55 and then increases at an increasing rate. In contrast to this, in the agriculture sector, the relationship of age with self-employment is very close to being linear as seen in Fig. 2.5a.

For people in the nonagriculture sector, the maps in Fig. 2.4 suggest that the north-south divide seen in the spatial effect on self-employment

[13] The structured spatial effects range from −0.8 to 0.8, the random unstructured local spatial effects range from −0.2 to 0.18.

[14] The parameters for a, b, the number of iterations, burnin, and the thinning parameter are set equal to the first model's parameters. The autocorrelation files and plots of the sampling paths show that sufficient convergence is achieved in these models also.

Table 2.4 Determinants of self-employment in nonagriculture (*Geoadditive model 2*)

Variable	Mean	Std. Dev.	2.5%-Qt.	97.5%-Qt.
Personal characteristics				
Female	−0.256	0.018	−0.290	−0.221
Married	0.203	0.019	0.165	0.240
Divorced	0.218	0.042	0.137	0.298
General education				
Informal	0.141	0.028	0.085	0.195
Primary school	0.130	0.021	0.086	0.169
High school	−0.039	0.022	−0.078	0.004
University	−0.349	0.024	−0.395	−0.301
Technical education				
Technical degree	−0.109	0.057	−0.217	0.004
Technical diploma	−0.134	0.025	−0.183	−0.084
Land possessed				
0.2 < land < 0.4 hectares	0.151	0.015	0.122	0.181
0.4 < land < 2 hectares	0.112	0.022	0.070	0.153
Land > 2 hectares	0.160	0.033	0.097	0.222
Location				
Urban	0.029	0.015	0.001	0.059
Religion & Social Group				
Hindu	−0.180	0.016	−0.213	−0.149
Backward	−0.150	0.014	−0.179	−0.121
Constant	−0.222	0.031	−0.282	−0.163
N	51674			
Deviance (Mean)	60166.724			
Std. Dev:	34.978124			
Deviance (μ)	59807.524			
pD	359.20045			
DIC	60525.925			

Notes: Dependent variable is binary self-employment status of the individual. Base categories for marital status, general education, technical education, land dummies are unmarried, no general education, no technical education and less than 0.2 hectares of land respectively. The confidence interval is given in the last two columns

for individuals in the first model is less pronounced. However, there are some significant spatial effects as seen in Fig. 2.4c. People of Kerala and some districts of Tamil Nadu in the south, Maharashtra and Madhya Pradesh in the western and central parts of India, and the majority of districts in the north-eastern states are less likely to be self-employed. In contrast to this, people living in Uttar Pradesh, Bihar, Rajasthan, and

Table 2.5 Determinants of self-employment in agriculture (*Geoadditive model 3*)

Variable	Mean	Std. Dev.	2.5%-Qt.	97.5%-Qt.
Personal characteristics				
Female	−0.540	0.027	−0.594	−0.487
Married	0.206	0.042	0.122	0.288
Divorced	0.447	0.058	0.336	0.558
General education				
Informal	0.233	0.032	0.164	0.296
Primary school	0.435	0.025	0.387	0.484
High school	0.758	0.035	0.689	0.827
University	0.862	0.076	0.722	1.018
Technical education				
Technical degree	0.157	0.274	−0.377	0.702
Technical diploma	0.193	0.114	−0.034	0.413
Land possessed				
0.2 < land < 0.4 hectares	0.533	0.042	0.443	0.614
0.4 < land < 2 hectares	1.986	0.042	1.903	2.074
Land > 2 hectares	2.787	0.050	2.686	2.892
Location				
Urban	0.459	0.044	0.378	0.543
Religion & Social Group				
Hindu	−0.015	0.035	−0.083	0.054
Backward	−0.286	0.027	−0.339	−0.235
Constant	−1.031	0.064	−1.155	−0.908
N	34466			
Deviance(Mean)	22493.237			
Std. Dev:	35.860231			
Deviance (μ)	22042.36			
pD	450.87693			
DIC	22944.114			

Notes: Dependent variable is binary self-employment status of the individual. Base categories for marital status, general education, technical education, land dummies are unmarried, no general education, no technical education and less than 0.2 hectares of land respectively. The confidence interval is given in the last two columns

some districts of Andhra Pradesh and West Bengal appear to be more likely to choose self-employment.

The maps of spatial effects in agriculture in Fig. 2.6 show many districts in the northern half of the map are white regions indicating that the impact of spatial location is significantly positive there, while most of the

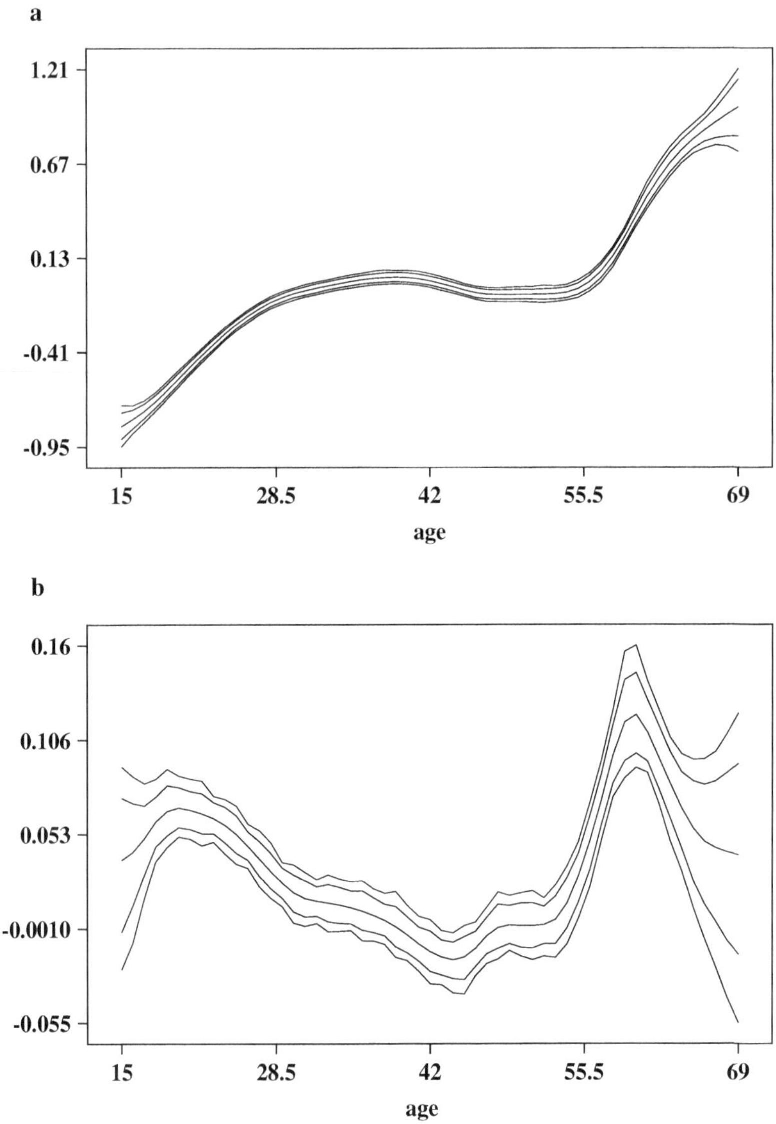

Fig. 2.3 Non-linear effect of age on self-employment in 'Nonagriculture' (*Geoadditive model 2*). (a) Posterior mean of the non-linear effect of 'age' together with 95% and 80% pointwise credible intervals in Nonagriculture. (b) Derivative of the posterior mean of the 'age' function with 95% and 80% pointwise credible intervals in Nonagriculture

(a)

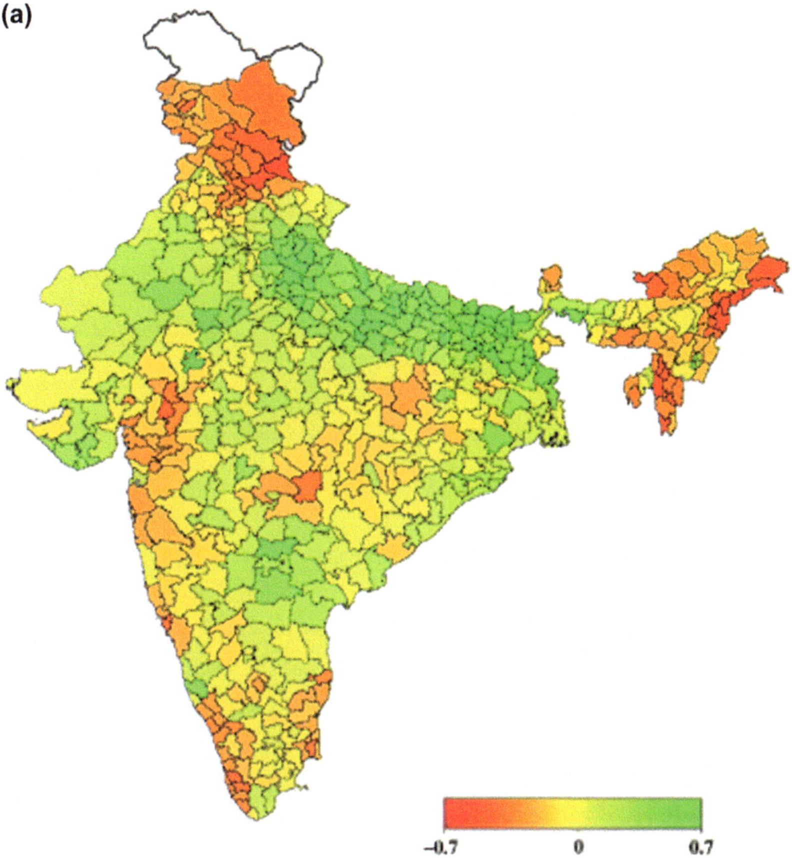

Fig. 2.4 Spatial effects in 'Nonagriculture' (*Geoadditive model 2*). (a) Structured non-linear effect of 'District' in nonagriculture. Shown are the posterior means. (b) Unstructured random effect of 'District' in nonagriculture. Shown are the posterior means. (c) Non-linear effect of 'District' in nonagriculture. Posterior probabilities for a nominal level of 95%. Black denotes regions with strictly negative credible intervals, and white denotes regions with strictly positive credible intervals. The white areas in Jammu and Kashmir are regions not included in the estimations. (d) Non-linear effect of 'District' in nonagriculture. Posterior probabilities for a nominal level of 80%. Black denotes regions with strictly negative credible intervals, and white denotes regions with strictly positive credible intervals. The white areas in Jammu and Kashmir are regions not included in the estimations

(b)

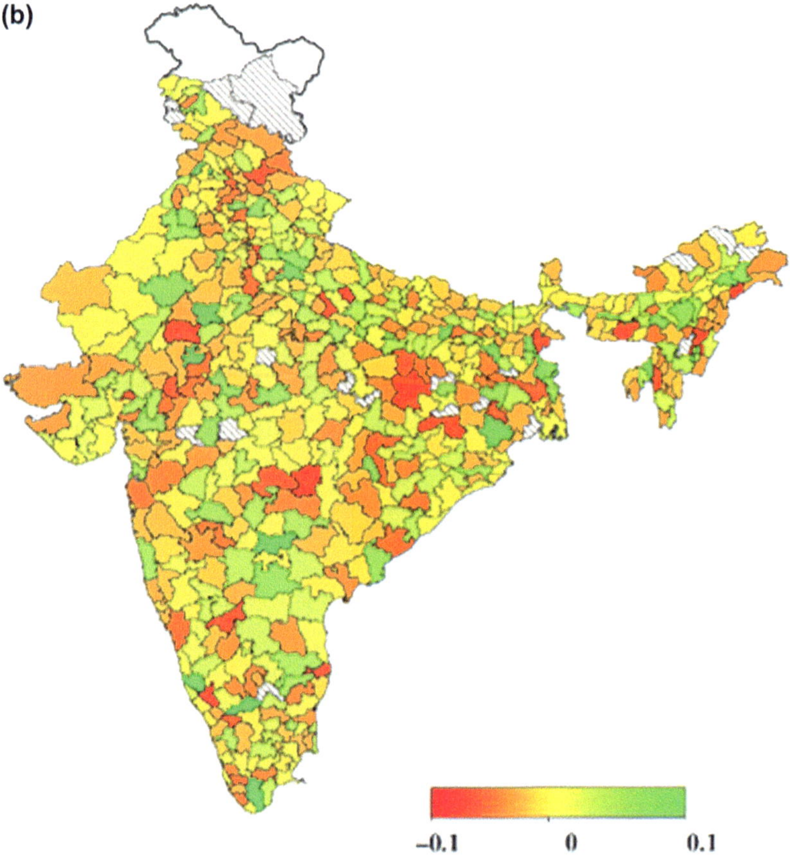

Fig. 2.4 (continued)

(c)

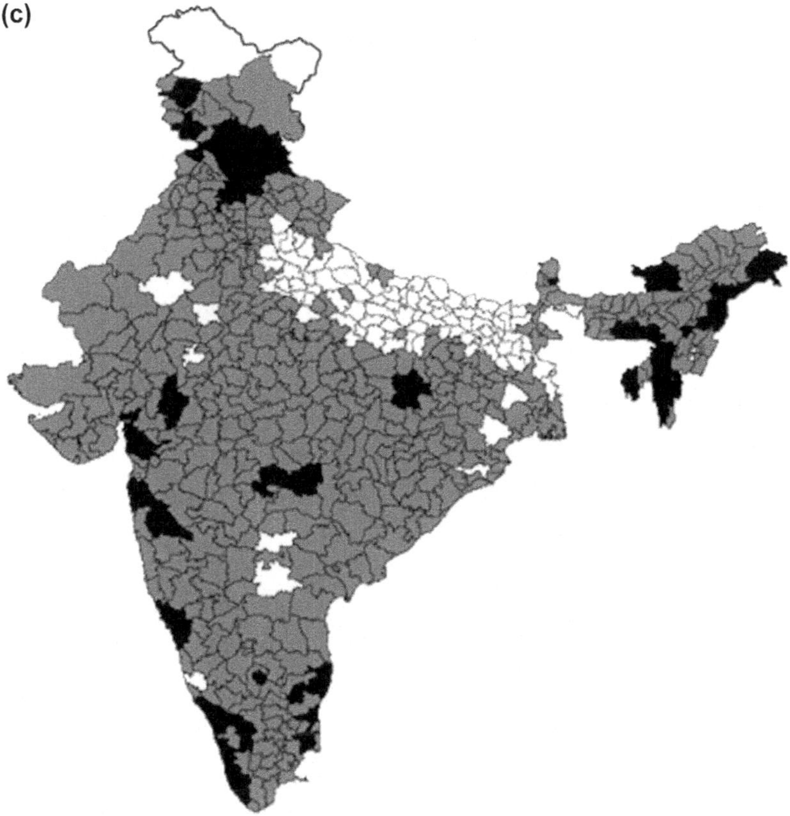

Fig. 2.4 (continued)

(d)

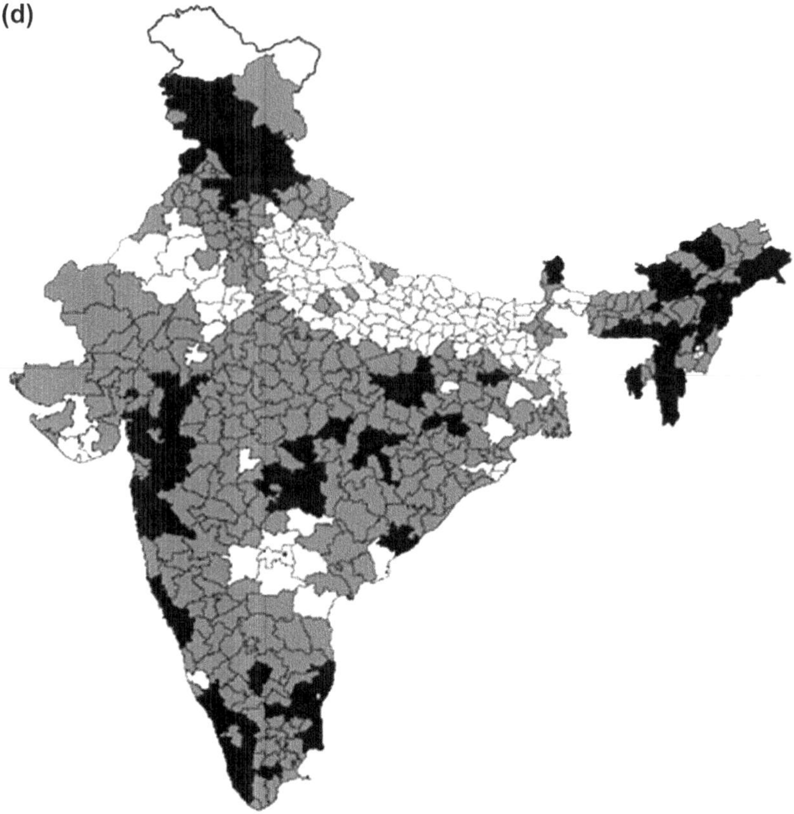

Fig. 2.4 (continued)

central and southern regions are black indicating that the impact of spatial location is significantly negative in these regions. Thus, the southern and central states are significantly less likely to have self-employment in agriculture when compared to the northern regions.

As Figs. 2.4b and 2.6b demonstrate, the unstructured random effects are negligible as compared to the structured spatial effects in both sectors. The confidence interval plots for the random spatial effects also show that these local effects are small and insignificant compared to the effects of structured spatial effects in all the three estimated models.

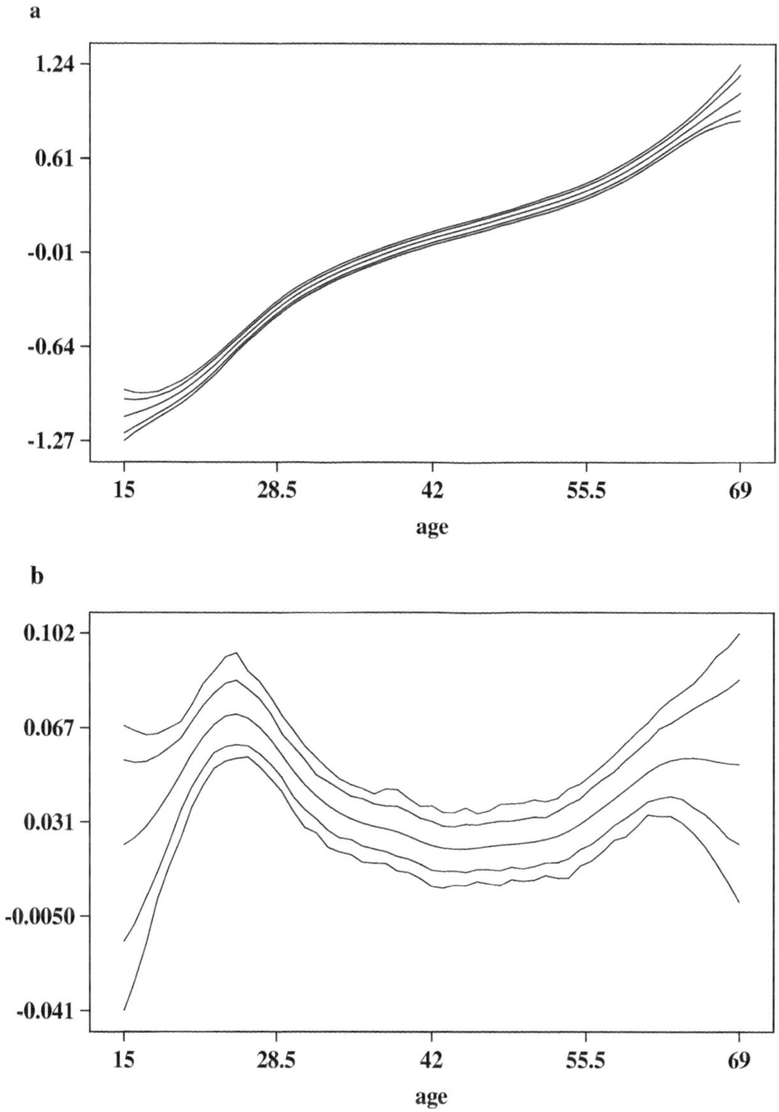

Fig. 2.5 Non-linear effects of age on self-employment in 'Agriculture' (*Geoadditive model 3*). (a) Posterior mean of the non-linear effect of 'age' together with 95% and 80% pointwise credible intervals in agriculture. (b) Derivative of the posterior mean of the 'age' function with 95% and 80% pointwise credible intervals in agriculture

(a)

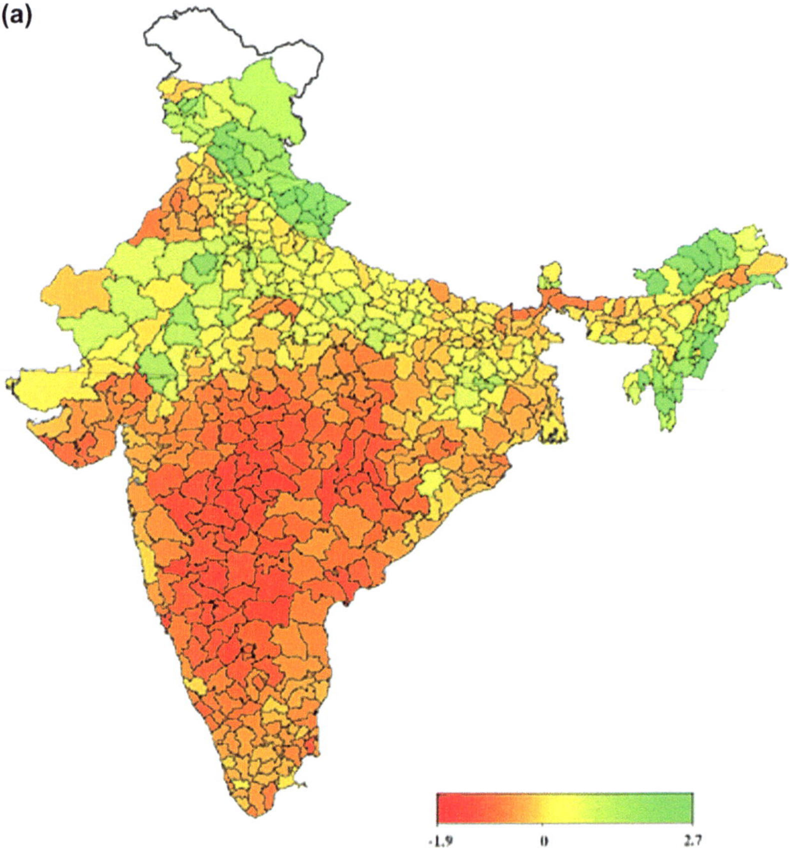

Fig. 2.6 Spatial effects in 'Agriculture' (*Geoadditive model 3*). (a) Structured non-linear effect of 'District' in agriculture. Shown are the posterior means. (b) Unstructured random effect of 'District' in agriculture. Shown are the posterior means. (c) Non-linear effect of 'District' in agriculture. Posterior probabilities for a nominal level of 95%. Black denotes regions with strictly negative credible intervals, and white denotes regions with strictly positive credible intervals. The white areas in Jammu and Kashmir are regions not included in the estimations. (d) Non-linear effect of 'District' in agriculture. Posterior probabilities for a nominal level of 80%. Black denotes regions with strictly negative credible intervals, and white denotes regions with strictly positive credible intervals. The white areas in Jammu and Kashmir are regions not included in the estimations

(b)

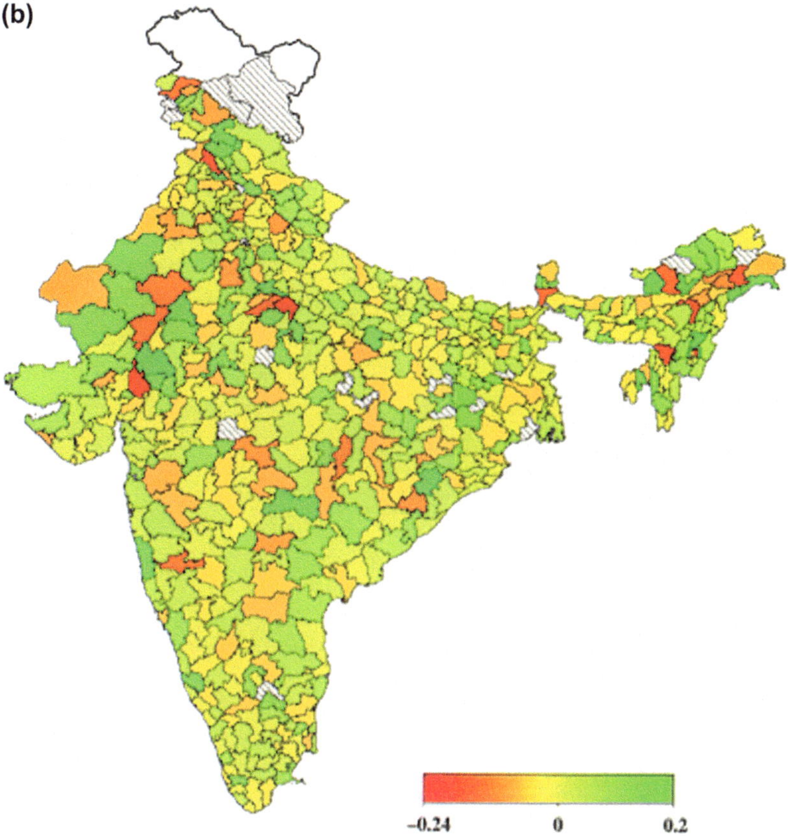

Fig. 2.6 (continued)

(c)

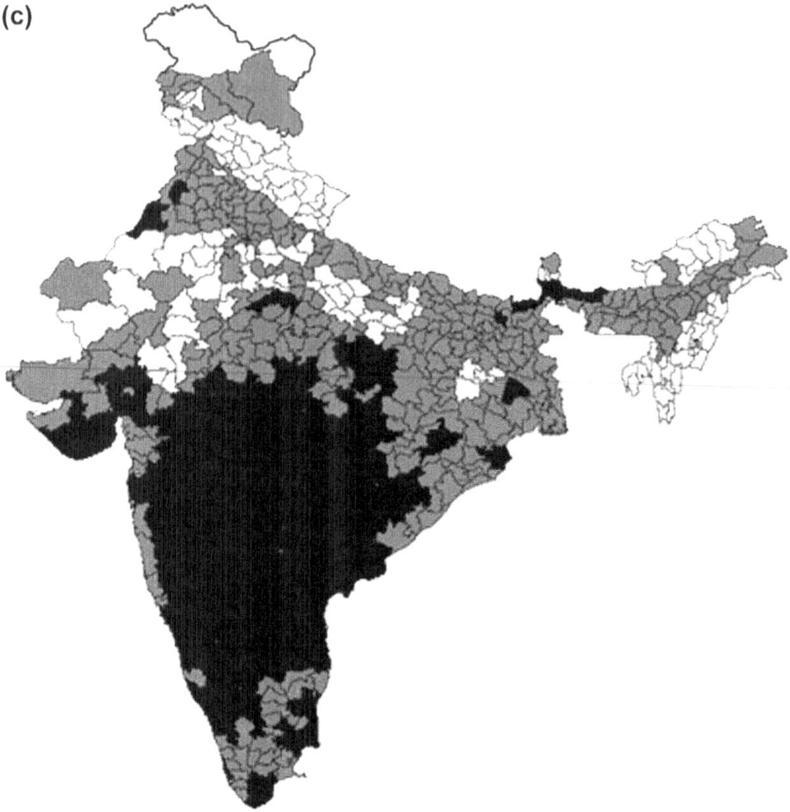

Fig. 2.6 (continued)

(d)

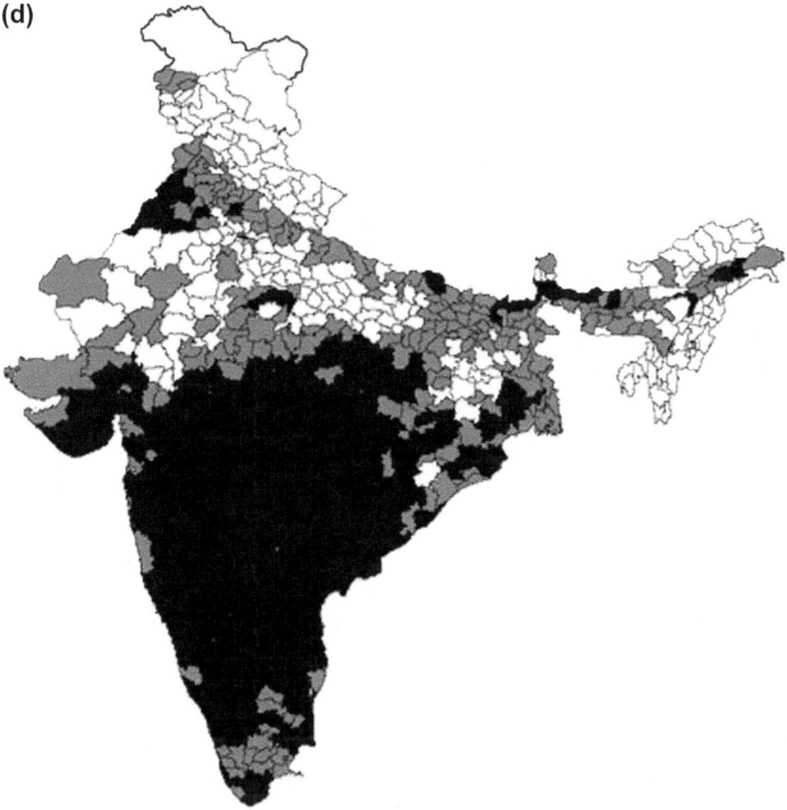

Fig. 2.6 (continued)

2.3.3 Explaining the Spatial Patterns

As individual characteristics are introduced into the geoadditive models along with spatial location, the estimated spatial patterns show the residual spatial patterns after filtering the effects of the individual characteristics. These estimated residual spatial patterns can be explained by regressing the mean residual spatial effects on the regional variables such as financial constraints, level of economic development, unemployment, and small business employment, as they are likely to have an influence on a regions' self-employment rates. Hence, these factors may explain the residual spatial patterns.

Firstly, many studies find that credit constraints are barriers to entry for individuals into self-employment (Blanchflower & Oswald, 1998; Evans & Jovanovic, 1989; Evans & Leighton, 1989b). Thus, the level of financial development in the region, proxied here by the per-capita credit or the credit-deposit ratio in a district, is likely to explain the residual spatial patterns to an extent.

Secondly, the residual spatial self-employment patterns can be attributed to the level of economic development in a region. For example, Lucas (1978) predicts that entrepreneurship will decrease with economic development. Calvo and Wellisz (1980) show that the growth rate of total stock of knowledge requires greater ability of the marginal entrepreneur in a steady-state equilibrium, suggesting that, for a given a fixed ability distribution in a population, the number of entrepreneurs decreases and average firm size increases with technological progress. Similarly, Acs, Audretsch, and Evans (1994) argue that self-employment decreases in the early stages of development as technological change shifts output from agriculture and small-scale industry to large-scale manufacturing.

Thirdly, regional unemployment rate may influence the spatial self-employment patterns. On the one hand, the recession-push hypothesis claims that high unemployment reduces the probability of obtaining paid employment and pushes individuals into self-employment, suggesting a positive relationship between unemployment and self-employment. On the other hand, the prosperity-pull hypothesis suggests that high unemployment reduces demand for goods and services provided by the self-employed, leading to a reduction in self-employment. In line with these, some studies find a positive relationship between unemployment and the probability of self-employment (Blanchflower & Meyer, 1994; Evans & Leighton, 1989b) while others find the opposite (Blanchflower & Oswald, 1998; Taylor, 1996).

Furthermore, following earlier studies, a number of other variables are considered here as potentially shaping the residual spatial patterns—in particular, the size of the district and its population density (Armington & Acs, 2002), and the level of agglomeration, measured by the density of firms in the region (Krugman, 1991).

In Table 2.6, the determinants of spatial variation in Figs. 2.2a, 2.4a, and 2.6a are estimated using the above set of regional indicators.[15] The dependent variables are the mean residual spatial effect in the district estimated by the three geoadditive models. The coefficient of the first proxy for financial development in Table 2.6, the per-capita credit, is insignificant for nonagriculture in column 3 as well as for agriculture in column 5. The coefficient of the second proxy, the credit-deposit ratio, is significant and positive in nonagriculture in column 4 and negative in agriculture in column 6. The level of economic development, measured by the per-capita net state domestic product, is negatively related to the probability of self-employment in both sectors in all the specifications. These observations support the claim of Acs et al. (1994) that technological change shifts output from agriculture and small-scale industry to large-scale manufacturing, resulting in a decrease in self-employment.

The results suggest that unemployment increases self-employment in nonagriculture, but is negatively related to self-employment in the agricultural sector.[16] Size of district and population density increase the

[15] The data on financial indicators for the regions, the per-capital net state domestic product (NSDP) come from the Reserve Bank of India's Handbook of Statistics on Indian Economy. The data on population density and size of the districts is taken from 2001 Census. The data on small firm density for constructing the agglomeration index are from the third census of small scale industries. The data on unemployment are based on the number of people registered at the employment exchanges.

[16] The unemployment rate in a district is constructed as the proportionate number of people in the district who have registered with the unemployment office. People registered with the unemployment office are mostly educated individuals looking for employment. In the absence of data on unemployment, this measure is used to proxy unemployment.

Table 2.6 Determinants of spatial patterns in Figs. 2.2, 2.4, and 2.6

	All		Nonagriculture		Agriculture	
Financial development						
Per-capita credit	0.00622		−0.0183		0.0275	
	(0.016)		(0.012)		(0.044)	
Credit-deposit ratio		−0.102***		0.0436**		−0.402***
		(0.023)		(0.018)		(0.061)
Economic development						
Per-capita NSDP	−0.310***	−0.268***	−0.291***	−0.325***	−0.418***	−0.253***
	(0.034)	(0.030)	(0.026)	(0.023)	(0.091)	(0.078)
Unemployment	−0.0603***	−0.0471***	0.0406***	0.0369***	−0.291***	−0.239***
	(0.016)	(0.015)	(0.012)	(0.012)	(0.041)	(0.040)
Demographics						
Mid-size district	0.00325	0.0141	0.0869***	0.0819***	−0.191**	−0.147*
	(0.030)	(0.029)	(0.022)	(0.022)	(0.079)	(0.076)
Large district	0.0280	0.0305	0.0750	0.0719	−0.176	−0.161
	(0.091)	(0.090)	(0.068)	(0.068)	(0.24)	(0.23)
Population density	−0.0189	−0.0183	0.0594***	0.0554***	−0.129***	−0.129***
	(0.015)	(0.014)	(0.011)	(0.011)	(0.040)	(0.037)
Agglomeration index						
Firm density	−0.00767	−0.00213	−0.00290	−0.00874	−0.0179	0.00453
	(0.013)	(0.012)	(0.0094)	(0.0090)	(0.033)	(0.031)
Constant	2.926***	2.534***	2.618***	2.749***	4.280***	2.778***
	(0.35)	(0.36)	(0.27)	(0.27)	(0.95)	(0.93)
Observations	534	534	531	531	532	532
R^2	0.20	0.23	0.40	0.40	0.16	0.22
F	19.08	22.46	49.43	50.30	14.11	21.42
R^2 Adjusted	0.192	0.220	0.390	0.394	0.147	0.212

Notes: *Signifies $p < 0.05$; ** Signifies $p < 0.01$; *** Signifies $p < 0.001$. Standard errors are reported in parentheses. Dependent variable is the mean spatial effect of a district after the estimation of the geoadditive models probability of self-employment in the nonagricultural sector but lower it in the agricultural sector. The negative sign in the agricultural sector may reflect the lesser availability of per-capita land, an important determinant of self-employment in agriculture.

The R-squared is 0.40 for both specifications explaining the residual spatial patterns of self-employment in the nonagricultural sector. However, the R-squared in the model explaining the residual spatial patterns of self-employment in agricultural sector is 0.16 when per-capita credit is included as a measure of financial development and 0.22 when the credit-deposit ratio is included as a measure of financial development. This suggests a better fit for the nonagricultural sector-a result attributable to the greater relevance of independent variables to the nonagricultural sector.[17]

2.4 Conclusion

In this chapter, geoadditive models are used to examine the role of spatial location, as well as individual characteristics, as determinants of self-employment choice in India. The empirical analysis suggests the presence of spatial occupational neighbourhoods and a clear north-south divide in self-employment choice when individuals from agricultural and nonagricultural sectors are considered together; however, such spatial patterns are less pronounced when individuals in nonagriculture alone are considered in the analysis. The analysis finds that in the nonagriculture sector, individuals in the northern states of Uttar Pradesh and Bihar have a significantly higher propensity to be self-employed.

The spatial effect is split into a spatially correlated and a spatially uncorrelated effect as it may comprise a component that has strong spatial structure and a component that is only locally present. The structured spatial effect models spatial dependence and estimates the impact of space as a continuous variate. Unlike the structured spatial effect, the

[17] The measure of agglomeration index, for instance, is more likely to explain the spatial pattern of self-employment in the nonagricultural sector than the spatial pattern in the agricultural sector.

unstructured spatial effect is localized and does not exhibit a spatial structure. This corresponds to the random component of the estimated spatial effects. The results presented in this chapter suggest that the structured spatial effect is stronger than the unstructured spatial effect in both agriculture and non-agriculture. Individuals in neighbouring regions are more likely to have similar occupational preferences, and people in some spatial neighbourhoods are more likely to be self-employed than those living elsewhere. Thus, there is clear evidence of neighbourhood effects and spatial continuity and dependence in self-employment choice.

These spatial patterns are influenced by the economic characteristics of the regions such as their level of economic development, financial accessibility, unemployment, and population density. In particular, in both sectors, self-employment is inversely related to the level of economic development suggesting that individuals are more likely to move out of self-employment as regions develop.

Appendix 1: Semiparametric Geo-additive Methodology

Geoadditive methodology based on semiparametric regression technique and Bayesian P-Splines is used for the empirical analysis. The methodology allows for the estimation of nonlinear effects of the continuous variables, such as age and spatial location, as well as individual characteristics, such as educational attainment, gender and marital status, on the probability of self-employment. As mentioned earlier, one of the main advantages of this method is that it allows simultaneous estimation of the effects of individual characteristics and spatial location on self-employment choice. Thus, the estimated spatial patterns reflect the propensity of people to be self-employed in a region after controlling for other individual-level effects and allow *ceteris paribus* interpretation. Furthermore, this method enables visual inspection of the estimated self-employment neighbourhoods. A brief outline of the method is presented below. This section draws on Lang and Brezger (2004) and Brezger and Lang (2005).

Geoadditive Models

Let (y_i, x_i, v_i) for i in $\{1, 2, \ldots \mathrm{N}\}$ describe a dataset of N observations. Let y_i be the response variable and x_i be a m-dimensional vector of continuous covariates and v_i be a vector of categorical variables. The case of the Gaussian response distribution is presented first, and then it is shown how the family of binomial probit models can be generalized to the family of Gaussian response, using a link function.

Assume y_i are independent and Gaussian with mean $\eta_i = f_1(x_{i1}) + \ldots + f_p(x_{ip}) + v_i\gamma$, and a common variance σ^2. If f_i are unknown smooth functions of the continuous variables and $v_i\gamma$ corresponds to the parametric part of the regression, the regression model is called an additive model or a semiparametric regressor. Eilers and Marx (1996) use polynomial regression splines that are parameterized in terms of B-spline basis functions, the P-splines, in the context of an additive model, to estimate the smooth functions within the semiparametric framework. Fahrmeir and Lang (2001a, 2001b) use simple random walk priors in a Bayesian version of the additive model. Kammann and Wand (2003) introduce geoadditive models within the additive mixed model framework to deal with unobserved heterogeneity across different spatial units. Furthermore, Lang and Brezger (2004) and Brezger and Lang (2005) generalize the work of Fahrmeir and Lang (2001a, 2001b) and develop the Bayesian version of the P-spline approach of Eilers and Marx (1996), Bayesian P-splines. These methods are used for the empirical analysis.

Assume that the unknown functions f_j can be approximated by a l degree spline with equally positioned knots in the domain of x_j (Eilers & Marx, 1996). By writing such a spline in the form of a linear combination of k B-spline basis functions B_{jk}, where k is equal to the number of knots plus the degree of the spline, $f_j(x_j) = \Sigma\beta_{jk}B_{jk}$ and, in matrix notation, $\eta = \Sigma X_j\beta_j + V\gamma$. By defining a roughness penalty based on the differences of adjacent B-spline coefficients, for ensuring smoothness of the estimated functions, the penalized likelihood assumes the form:

$$L = l\left(y,\beta_1,\ldots,\beta_p,\gamma\right) - \lambda_1 \Sigma\left(\Delta^k \beta_1\right)^2 - \ldots \lambda_p \Sigma\left(\Delta^k \beta_p\right)^2 \tag{2.1}$$

In the Bayesian framework, β_j for $j = 1\ldots p$ and γ are considered random variables and assigned prior distributions. Independent diffuse priors are assumed for the fixed effects parameters, $\gamma_j \propto const$ for $j = 1\ldots q$. The priors for the coefficients of the nonlinear functions β_j, are obtained by substituting the stochastic analogues of the difference penalties. In case of first differences, a first-order random walk and, for second differences, a second-order random walk, are considered. Hence, $\beta_{jk} = \beta_{j,k-1} + u_{jk}$ or $\beta_{jk} = 2\beta_{j,k-1} - \beta_{j,k-2} + u_{jk}$ with Gaussian errors $u_{jk} \sim N\left(0,\tau_j^2\right)$ and constant diffuse priors for the initial values of β_{j1} and β_{j2}. τ_j^2 controls the smoothness of the fitted function. For Bayesian inference, τ_j^2 are also treated as random variables and simultaneously estimated with the β_j. Highly dispersed inverse gamma priors $IG(a_j, b_j)$ are assigned to the variances τ_j^2.

The geoadditive model is obtained when a spatial effect, f_{spatial}, is added to the above predictor. The spatial effect may be split into spatially correlated and uncorrelated effects $f_{\text{spatial}} = f_{\text{str}} + f_{\text{unstr}} = X_{\text{str}}\beta_{\text{str}} + X_{\text{unstr}}\beta_{\text{untr}}$, as the spatial effect may comprise a component that has strong spatial structure and a component that is only locally present. Following Besag, York, and Molli (1991). Markov random field (MRF) priors are assumed for the regression coefficients β_{str}. If $s \in 1, \ldots S$ are pixels of a lattice or regions of a geographical map, the MRF prior is given as,

$$\frac{\beta_{str,s}}{\beta_{str,u}} \sim N\left(\sum_{u\in\partial_s} \frac{1}{N_s}\beta_{str,u}, \frac{\tau_{str}^2}{N_s}\right) \tag{2.2}$$

for $u \neq s$, where, N_s is the number of adjacent regions (pixels) and ∂_s is the neighbourhood of s. This prior may be seen as an extension of a first-order random walk into two dimensional space. For the second component β_{unstr}, independent and identically distributed (i.i.d.) Gaussian random priors $\beta_{\text{unstr}}(s) \sim N(0, \tau^2_{\text{unstr}})$, are assumed for s = 1…, S. For τ^2_{str} and τ^2_{unstr} inverse gamma priors, $IG(a_{\text{str}}, b_{\text{str}})$ and $IG(a_{\text{unstr}}, b_{\text{unstr}})$ are assumed.

Inference is based on the posterior and employs recent Monte Carlo Markov Chain (MCMC) techniques. If α is a vector of the unknown parameters, assuming conditional independence of the parameters, the posterior is given by:

$$p\left(\frac{\alpha}{y}\right) \propto L\left(y, \beta_1, \ldots, \beta_p, \beta_{\text{str}}, \beta_{\text{unstr}}, \gamma, \sigma^2\right) \times \prod_{j=1}^{p} \left(p\left(\frac{\beta_j}{\tau_j^2}\right) p\left(\tau_j^2\right) \right)$$
$$\times p\left(\frac{\beta_{\text{str}}}{\tau^2_{\text{str}}}\right) p\left(\tau^2_{\text{str}}\right) p\left(\frac{\beta_{\text{unstr}}}{\tau^2_{\text{unstr}}}\right) p(\gamma) p\left(\sigma^2\right)$$

The probit model in this setting, where y_i assumes only binary values 0 or 1, requires slight modifications of the posterior. Here y_i follows Bernoulli distribution $y_i \sim B(1, \mu_i)$, conditional on the covariates and parameters. The mean $\mu_i = \Phi(\eta_i)$ where Φ is the cumulative normal distribution function. Consider the latent variables $U_i = \eta_i + \epsilon_i$ with $\epsilon_i \sim N(0, 1)$. By defining $y_i = 1$ if $U_i \geq 0$ and $y_i = 0$ otherwise, the model corresponds to a binary probit model. The new posterior also depends on the extra parameters of the latent variable U_i.

Model Diagnostics

Following Spiegelhalter, Best, Carlin, and Van Der Linde (2002), the deviance information criteria (DIC) is used as a measure of complexity and fit for model selection. The DIC is defined as the "classical estimate of fit, plus twice the effective number of parameters" (Spiegelhalter et al., 2002, p. 603). The unstandardized deviance is given by $-2\ log\ \{p(y/\mu)\}$. Assuming $f(y)$ as a standardizing term that is a function of the data alone, the classical estimate of fit, $D(\bar{\theta})$ is obtained from $D(\theta) = -2\ log\ \{p(y/\theta)\} + 2 log f(y)$, by evaluating $D(\theta)$ at the mean of the parameters $\bar{\theta}$. $D(\theta)$ is also referred to as the Bayesian deviance or the saturated deviance. For members of the exponential family with $E(Y) = \mu(\theta)$, $D(\theta)$ is obtained by setting $f(y) = p\{y/\mu(\theta) = y\}$. That is, $D(\theta) = -2\ log\ \{p(y/\theta)\} + 2\ log\ \{p(y/\mu(\theta) = y)\}$. The measure of the effective number of parameters, p_D, is the difference between the posterior mean of deviance $\overline{D(\theta)}$ and deviance at the posterior means of the parameters $D(\bar{\theta})$. That is, if $p_D = \overline{D(\theta)} - D(\bar{\theta})$, then $DIC = D(\bar{\theta}) + 2p_D = \overline{D(\theta)} + p_D$. Of the competing models, the specification with the least DIC is selected and reported.

References

Acs, Z. J., Audretsch, D. B., & Evans, D. S. (1994). *Why does self employment rate vary across countries and over time.* CEPR Discussion Paper no. 871. Center for Economic Policy Research, London.

Anselin, L. (1988). *Spatial econometrics: Methods and models*. Kluwer.

Armington, C., & Acs, Z. J. (2002). The determinants of regional variation in new firm formation. *Regional Studies, 36*, 33–45.

Audretsch, D. B., Boente, W., & Tamvada, J. P. (2013). Religion, social class, and entrepreneurial choice. *Journal of Business Venturing, 28*(6), 774–789.

Banerjee, A. V., & Neuman, A. F. (1993). Occupational choice and the process of economic development. *Journal of Political Economy, 101*, 274–298.

Besag, J., York, J., & Molli, A. (1991). Bayesian image restoration with two applications in spatial statistics. *Annals of Institute of Statistical Mathematics, 43*, 1–59.

Blanchflower, D. G. (2000). Self-employment in OECD countries. *Labour Economics, 7*(5), 471–505.

Blanchflower, D. G., & Meyer, B. D. (1994). A longitudinal analysis of young entrepreneurs in Australia and the United States. *Small Business Economics, 6*(1), 1–19.

Blanchflower, D. G., & Oswald, A. (1998). What makes an entrepreneur? *Journal of Labor Economics, 16*(1), 26–60.

Blau, D. M. (1986). Self-employment, earnings, and mobility in peninsular Malaysia. *World Development, 14*(7), 839–852.

Bohacek, R. (2006). Financial constraints and entrepreneurial investment. *Journal of Monetary Economics, 53*(8), 2195–2212.

Borjas, G. J. (1986). The self-employment experience of immigrants. *The Journal of Human Resources, 21*(4), 485–506.

Borjas, G. J., & Bronars, S. G. (1989). Consumer discrimination and self employment. *Journal of Political Economy, 97*, 581–605.

Brezger, A., & Lang, S. (2005). Generalised structured additive regression based on Bayesian p-splines. *Computational Statistics and Data Analysis, 50*(4), 967–991.

Calvo, G., & Wellisz, S. (1980). Technology, entrepreneurs, and firm size. *The Quarterly Journal of Economics, 95*(4), 663–677.

Carroll, C. D. (2000). *Portfolios of the rich*. NBER Working Paper.

Chiswick, C. U. (1976). On estimating earnings functions for LDCs. *Journal of Development Economics, 3*(1), 67–78.

Cunningham, W. V., & Maloney, W. F. (2001). Heterogeneity in the Mexican micro-enterprise sector. *Economic Development and Cultural Change, 50*, 131–156.

Eilers, P. H. C., & Marx, B. D. (1996). Flexible smoothing using B-splines and penalized likelihood. *Statistical Science, 11*(2), 89–121.

Evans, D. S., & Jovanovic, B. (1989). An estimated model of entrepreneurial choice under liquidity constraints. *Journal of Political Economy, 97*(4), 808–827.

Evans, D. S., & Leighton, L. S. (1989a). The determinants of changes in US self-employment, 1968–1987. *Small Business Economics, 1*, 111–119.

Evans, D. S., & Leighton, L. S. (1989b). Some empirical aspects of entrepreneurship. *American Economic Review, 79*(3), 519–535.

Fahrmeir, L., & Kneib, T. (2011). *Bayesian smoothing and regression for longitudinal, spatial and event history data*. Oxford University Press.

Fahrmeir, L., & Lang, S. (2001a). Bayesian inference for generalised additive mixed models based on Markov random field priors. *Journal of the Royal Statistical Society C(Applied Statistics), 50*, 201–220.

Fahrmeir, L., & Lang, S. (2001b). Bayesian semiparametric regression analysis of multicategorical time-space data. *Annals of the Institute of Statistical Mathematics, 53*, 10–30.

Fairlie, R. W., & Meyer, B. D. (1996). Ethnic and racial self-employment: Differences and possible explanations. *Journal of Human Resources, 31*(4), 757–793.

Fields, G. S. (2005). *A guide to multisector labor market models*. Social Protection Discussion Paper Series No. 0505, World Bank.

Foelster, S. (2002). Do lower taxes stimulate self-employment? *Small Business Economics, 19*(2), 135–145.
Fuchs, V. R. (1982). Self-employment and labor force participation of older males. *The Journal of Human Resources, 17*(3), 339–357.
Georgellis, Y., & Wall, H. J. (2000). What makes a region more entrepreneurial? evidence from Britain. *Annals of Regional Science, 34*, 385–403.
Gindling, T. H. (1991). Labor market segmentation and the determination of wages in the public, private-formal and informal sectors in San Jose, Costa Rica. *Economic Development and Cultural Change, 39*, 585–605.
Glaeser E. L. (2007). *Entrepreneurship and the city.* Working Paper No.13551, National Bureau of Economic Research, Cambridge, MA
Goedhuys, M., & Sleuwaegen, L. (2000). Entrepreneurship and growth of entrepreneurial firms in Cote d' Ivoire. *Journal of Development Studies, 36*, 122–145.
Guenther, I., & Launov, A. (2006). Competitive and segmented informal labor markets. IZA Discussion Papers 2349, Institute for the Study of Labor (IZA).
Harris, J. R., & Todaro, M. P. (1970). Migration, unemployment and development: A two sector analysis. *American Economic Review, 60*(1), 126–142.
Hurst, E., & Lusardi, A. (2004). Liquidity constraints, household wealth, and entrepreneurship. *Journal of Political Economy, 112*(2), 319–347.
Iyigun, M. F., & Owen, A. L. (1999). Entrepreneurs, professionals, and growth. *Journal of Economic Growth, 4*, 213–232.
Johnson, W. (1978). A theory of job shipping. *Quarterly Journal of Economics, 22*, 261–278.
Jovanovic, B. (1979). Job matching and the theory of turnover. *The Journal of Political Economy, 87*(5), 972–990.
Kammann, E. E., & Wand, M. P. (2003). Geoadditive models. *Journal of the Royal Statistical Society C, 52*, 1–18.
Kihlstrom, R. E., & Laffont, J. J. (1979). A general equilibrium entrepreneurial theory of firm formation based on risk aversion. *Journal of Political Economy, 87*, 719–748.
Krugman, P. (1991). Increasing returns and economic geography. *Journal of Political Economy, 99*(3), 483–499.
Lang, S., & Brezger, A. (2004). Bayesian p-splines. *Journal of Computational and Graphical Statistics, 13*, 183–212.
Lesage, J., & Pace, R. (2009). *Introduction to spatial econometrics.* Chapman & Hall/CRC Press.
Lewis, A. W. (1954). *Economic development with unlimited supplies of Labour.* Manchester: University of Manchester.

Lucas, R. (1978). On the size distribution of business firms. *Bell Journal of Economics, 9*, 508–523.
Magnac, T. (1991). Segmented or competitive labor markets. *Econometrica, 59*, 165–187.
Majumdar, D. (1981). *The urban labor market and income distribution—A study of Malaysia*. Oxford University Press.
Maloney, W. F. (2004). Informality revisited. *World Development, 32*(7), 1159–1178.
Miller, R. (1984). Job matching and occupational choice. *Journal of Political Economy, 92*, 1086–1120.
Mohapatra, S., Rozelle, S., & Goodhue, R. (2007). The rise of self-employment in rural China: Development or distress? *World Development, 35*(1), 163–181.
Parker, S. C. (2005). Explaining regional variations in entrepreneurship as multiple occupational equilibria. *Journal of Regional Science, 45*(4), 829–850.
Parker, S. C. (2018). *The economics of entrepreneurship*. Cambridge University Press.
Pratap, S., & Quintin, E. (2006). Are labor markets segmented in developing countries? A semiparametric approach. *European Economic Review, 50*, 1817–1841.
Quinn, J. F. (1980). Labor-force participation patterns of older self-employed workers. *Social Security Bulletin, 43*(4), 17–28.
Ranis, G., & Fei, J. (1961). A theory of economic development. *American Economic Review, 51*, 533–565.
Robson, M. T. (1998). Self-employment in the UK regions. *Applied Economics, 30*, 313–322.
Rosenzweig, M. R. (1980). Neoclassical theory and the optimizing peasant: An econometric analysis of market family labour supply in a developing country. *Quarterly Journal of Economics, 94*(1), 31–55.
Sen, A. K. (1966). Peasants and dualism with or without surplus labor. *Journal of Political Economy, 74*, 425–450.
Sluis, J. V. D., Van Praag, M., & Vijverberg, W. (2005). Entrepreneurship selection and performance: A meta-analysis of the impact of education in developing economies. *World Bank Economic Review, 2*, 225–261.
Spiegelhalter, D. J., Best, N. G., Carlin, B. P., & Van Der Linde, A. (2002). Bayesian measures of model complexity and fit. *Journal of the Royal Statistical Society: Series B (Statistical Methodology), 64*(2), 583–639.
Taylor, M. P. (1996). Earnings, independence or unemployment: Why become self-employed? *Oxford Bulletin of Economics and Statistics, 58*, 253–266.

Torrini, R. (2005). Cross-country differences in self-employment rates: The role of institutions. *Labour Economics, 12*(5), 661–683.
Van Praag, C. M., & Cramer, J. S. (2001). The roots of entrepreneurship and labour demand: Individual ability and low risk aversion. *Economica, 68*(269), 45–62.
Yamada, G. (1996). Urban informal employment and self-employment in developing countries: Theory and evidence. *Economic Development and Cultural Change, 44*, 289–314.

3

Economic Returns to Occupational Choice

3.1 Background

A rich literature provides insights into the determinants of entrepreneurship and its economic returns.[1] According to the expected utility theory, individuals choose self-employment when they expect higher returns from doing so relative to wage-employment (Rees & Shaw, 1986). In contrast, according to the non-pecuniary benefits theory, people select into entrepreneurship, even if the expected returns are lower, in search of non-pecuniary benefits, such as being their own boss (Hamilton, 2000). However, entrepreneurs are not a homogenous group of individuals, and the type of entrepreneurship engaged in may have a significant effect on the returns.[2]

While many models in the economics of entrepreneurship assume that individuals become self-employed as they expect higher returns relative to wage employment (Blau, 1987; Parker, 1996; Rees & Shaw, 1986), the labour and development literature suggests that people are forced into

[1] See Parker (2018) for a synthesis of this literature.

[2] For example, while some entrepreneurs employ others, the rest are solely self-employed individuals

J. P. Tamvada, *Microentrepreneurship in a Developing Country*,
https://doi.org/10.1007/978-3-030-68628-4_3

self-employment in the absence of viable economic opportunities in developing countries. However, some scholars believe that the self-employment sector consists of both voluntarily self-selected competitive workers as well as disadvantaged individuals (Cunningham & Maloney, 2001; Fields, 2005; Gindling, 1991; Günther & Launov, 2006; Magnac, 1991; Maloney, 2004).[3]

In this context, for a given occupational structure of individuals in an economy, the returns to occupations are likely to depend on the relative positioning of individuals in the welfare distribution. Self-employed individuals at the lower end of the distribution fundamentally differ from the self employed individuals in the upper end of the distribution. This is also true for salaried employees. Occupations and their economic returns are characterized by a heterogeneity that is not discernable in studies that examine this relationship solely at the mean. For testing this hypothesis of heterogeneous returns of occupation across the welfare distribution, we employ quantile regressions (see Koenker & Hallock, 2001, and references therein) here. By examining the returns to occupations across the welfare distribution, we assess the relative returns to occupations in greater detail.

The superstar model of Rosen (1981) suggests that a comparison of the mean earnings of workers in self-employed sector and in wage sector would be highly influenced by a few entrepreneurial superstars, and mean earnings do not really characterize the returns of the majority of self-employed individuals. The greatest advantage of using quantile regressions is their ability to show snapshots of relationships across different quantiles of the distribution and not only at the mean. Most studies use income measures to examine the returns of occupations (Hamilton, 2000). We use consumption measures here as income is usually highly correlated with consumption (Browning & Lusardi, 1996), and an analysis of the consumption patterns itself has the advantage that variation is not as high as in income data.[4]

[3] Pratap and Quintin (2006) argue that there is no evidence of market segmentation in the labour markets of developing countries.

[4] However, as people with higher incomes are likely to have greater savings, an analysis of the consumption patterns for welfare comparisons may make their returns appear flattened to some extent.

3.2 Occupations and Their Returns in India

The data used for the analysis once again originate from the 60th round employment–unemployment survey of the National Sample Survey Organization (NSSO) of India. We only consider those households where the household heads are reported to be self-employed (includes own account workers and employers), salaried employees, casual labourers, and unemployed. The sample is restricted to those who are older than 15 years but younger than 70 years. We then consider only those households who work in the nonagriculture sectors. The final sample consists of 26,485 households, of which only the household head is economically active in 13,782 households.

Table 3.1 reports summary statistics of the database. The first two data columns report the mean and standard deviation of the variables when the when the entire database is considered. The third and fourth columns report the descriptive statistics when the database is restricted to households that have the household head as the sole economically active member. As the descriptive data on monthly per-capita consumption expenditure (MPCE) in columns 1 and 3 show, employers have the highest average consumption rate. The self-employed individuals have a consumption rate that is lower than that of salaried employees but higher than the consumption rate of the casual labourers. Figure 3.1 shows that kernel density plots of log per-capita consumption of households with heads working as self-employed, salaried employees, employers, and labourers. The distribution plots of salaried employees and employers are to the right of the self-employed, and the density of the labourers is centred to their left. The plots also show that the inequality observed in the employer group is substantially higher than that in the other groups.

Table 3.1 Summary statistics

	Households		Household Heads	
Variables	Mean	SD	Mean	SD
Consumption				
Log (MPCE-All)	6.63	0.63	6.71	0.64
Log (MPCE-Employers)	7.27	0.58	7.29	0.59
Log (MPCE-Salaried)	6.84	0.61	6.92	0.61
Log (MPCE-Self-employed)	6.52	0.59	6.59	0.60
Log(MPCE-Labourers)	6.25	0.47	6.28	0.50
Occupation				
Self-employed	0.40	0.49	0.37	0.48
Employers	0.01	0.12	0.02	0.12
Salaried employees	0.42	0.49	0.47	0.50
Labourer	0.16	0.36	0.15	0.35
Unemployed	0.01	0.09	0.01	0.08
Personal characteristics				
Age	41.96	10.71	38.36	9.69
Female	0.05	0.22	0.05	0.22
Married	0.90	0.30	0.89	0.31
Divorce/Widow	0.05	0.22	0.04	0.20
Education				
Informal Education	0.09	0.28	0.07	0.26
Primary school	0.32	0.47	0.31	0.46
High school	0.26	0.44	0.29	0.45
University education	0.16	0.37	0.20	0.40
Technical degree or diploma	0.07	0.25	0.08	0.27
Household variables				
Prop. children (less 5 years)	0.10	0.15	0.12	0.17
Prop. children (6–10 years)	0.09	0.14	0.11	0.16
Prop. children (11–15 years)	0.09	0.14	0.10	0.15
Prop. females (15–60 years)	0.32	0.17	0.30	0.19
Prop. males (15–60 years)	0.39	0.22	0.37	0.25
Prop. old (above 60 years)	0.01	0.05	0.01	0.05
Urban	0.59	0.49	0.62	0.49
Land Code 1	0.35	0.48	0.40	0.49
Land Code 2	0.53	0.50	0.52	0.50
Land Code 3	0.09	0.29	0.07	0.25
Land Code 4	0.02	0.15	0.01	0.12
Household size	4.80	2.31	4.00	1.76
Manufacturing	0.22	0.41	0.21	0.41
Trade	0.21	0.41	0.20	0.40
Service	0.26	0.44	0.27	0.45
Public	0.18	0.38	0.19	0.39

Notes: The first two columns report the mean and standard deviation of variables in the samples. The third and fourth columns report the mean and standard deviation when the sample is restricted to those households where the household head is the only economically active individual

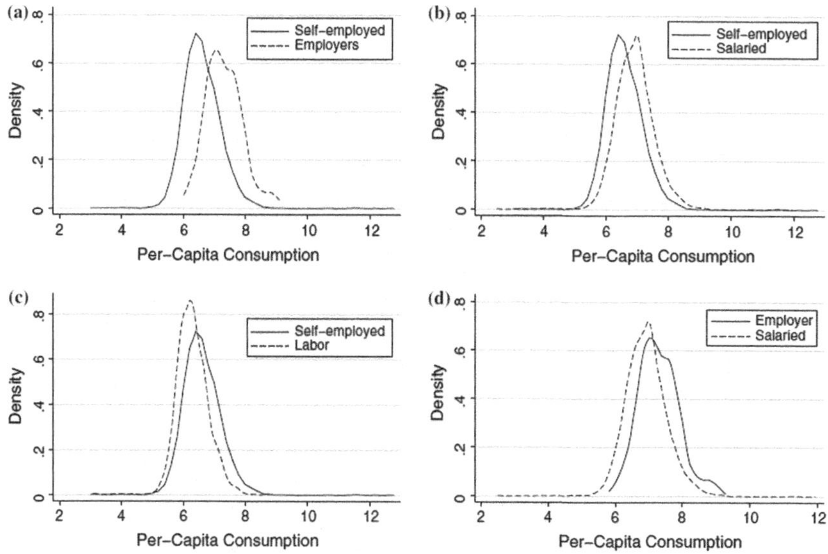

Fig. 3.1 Consumption and occupation (Un-normalized)

3.2.1 Household Level Analysis

The paths of consumption and income closely follow one another when the latter has some persistence (Browning & Lusardi, 1996).[5] Here the log of per-capita consumption of households is used as the dependent variable in the estimations.

The occupations of the members of the household enter the estimations as independent variables along with a series of controls including personal characteristics of the household head, demographics of the household, educational background of the members, urban location, and land possessed, as they are likely to influence the per-capita consumption

[5] Other studies use per-capita consumption (Wodon, 2000). Many alternate strategies to construct welfare measures that are comparable across households exist. For instance, Lazear and Michael (1980) develop a technique that converts families of different structures into single person equivalents. Also see Muellbauer (1974) and Deaton and Muellbauer (1980, 1986) for a theory of equivalence scales.

of the households.[6] A potential source of endogeneity may arise as personal characteristics, such as age and educational background of the household members also determine their occupational choice. However, the chapter's main aim is to examine if a welfare hierarchy of occupations is present across the welfare distribution, conditional on holding individual as well as household characteristics constant. This issue of endogeneity addressed using multinomial selection models does not give qualitatively different results.

The third and fourth columns of Table 3.1 report the descriptive statistics when the database is restricted to households that have the household head as the sole economically active member. As the descriptive data on monthly per-capita consumption expenditure (MPCE) in columns 1 and 3 show, employers have the highest average consumption rate. Self-employed individuals have a consumption rate that is lower than that of salaried employees but higher than the consumption rate of the casual labourers. Figure 3.1 shows that kernel density plots of log per- capita consumption of households with heads working as self-employed, salaried employees, employers, and labourers. While the distribution plots of salaried employees and employers are to the right of the self-employed individuals, the density of the labourers is centred to their left. The plots also show that the inequality observed in the employer group is substantially higher than that in the other groups.

The results presented in Table 3.2 suggest that the entrepreneurship has a distinct relationship with welfare. As mentioned earlier, people in the database belong to one of the five primary occupations—they are either employers, self-employed, salaried employees, casual labourers, or unemployed. In this estimation, the category that is left out of the occupation variables is the proportion of economically active individuals in a household who are self-employed. As the positive coefficients suggest, households that have a higher proportion of employers and those that a higher proportion of salaried employees have higher per-capita consumption levels than self-employed households. However, households that have a higher proportion of casual labourers and unemployed people

[6] Land variables proxy the wealth of the household. Wodon (2000) suggests that the land possessed by a household is also a determinant of the welfare.

Table 3.2 Households, occupation and consumption (*Estimates of simultaneous quantile regression*)

Independent Var.	q10	q25	q50	q75	q90
Occupation					
Prop. employers	0.336***	0.342***	0.405***	0.454***	0.461***
	(0.038)	(0.047)	(0.039)	(0.035)	(0.045)
Prop. salaried	0.0816***	0.0945***	0.0996***	0.0841***	0.0778***
	(0.011)	(0.0081)	(0.0077)	(0.0069)	(0.013)
Prop. labourers	−0.148***	−0.143***	−0.158***	−0.172***	−0.184***
	(0.012)	(0.011)	(0.010)	(0.012)	(0.016)
Prop. unemployed	−0.192***	−0.187***	−0.208***	−0.242***	−0.182***
	(0.032)	(0.017)	(0.027)	(0.020)	(0.043)
Head's characteristics					
Age	0.0164***	0.0162***	0.0184***	0.0204***	0.0163***
	(0.0038)	(0.0019)	(0.0016)	(0.0026)	(0.0050)
Age square	−0.0163***	−0.0156***	−0.0174***	−0.0193***	−0.0146**
	(0.0042)	(0.0022)	(0.0018)	(0.0032)	(0.0057)
Female	−0.0912***	−0.0896***	−0.0738***	−0.0801***	−0.0573**
	(0.025)	(0.025)	(0.014)	(0.021)	(0.025)
Married	0.0516*	0.0459***	0.0495***	0.0261	0.00218
	(0.028)	(0.017)	(0.016)	(0.025)	(0.031)
Divorce/widow	−0.0382	−0.0242	−0.0285	−0.0162	−0.0205
	(0.042)	(0.026)	(0.025)	(0.030)	(0.044)
Education					
Prop. informal education	0.196***	0.200***	0.220***	0.214***	0.238***
	(0.022)	(0.012)	(0.010)	(0.017)	(0.033)
Prop. primary school	0.343***	0.344***	0.365***	0.381***	0.422***
	(0.021)	(0.014)	(0.013)	(0.017)	(0.024)
Prop. high school	0.565***	0.602***	0.661***	0.704***	0.758***
	(0.024)	(0.017)	(0.018)	(0.019)	(0.028)
Prop. university education	0.958***	1.072***	1.187***	1.335***	1.519***
	(0.019)	(0.020)	(0.020)	(0.032)	(0.031)
Prop. technical degree	0.190***	0.235***	0.253***	0.281***	0.305***
	(0.020)	(0.017)	(0.033)	(0.038)	(0.035)
Demographics					
Prop. children (less 5 years)	−0.133***	−0.0732***	−0.0156	0.00982	0.0198
	(0.025)	(0.023)	(0.032)	(0.027)	(0.053)
Prop. children (6–10 years)	−0.125***	−0.0638**	0.0116	0.0301	0.0981*
	(0.036)	(0.025)	(0.028)	(0.037)	(0.052)
Prop. children (11–15 years)	−0.140***	−0.0941***	−0.0601*	−0.0500*	−0.0402
	(0.035)	(0.022)	(0.032)	(0.027)	(0.048)

(*continued*)

Table 3.2 (continued)

Independent Var.	q10	q25	q50	q75	q90
Prop. females (15–60 years)	0.000581	0.0323	0.0442**	0.0604**	0.0900**
	(0.020)	(0.021)	(0.018)	(0.025)	(0.039)
Prop. old (above 60 years)	0.188***	0.196***	0.212***	0.336***	0.383***
	(0.067)	(0.041)	(0.060)	(0.082)	(0.11)
Household characteristics					
Urban	0.232***	0.233***	0.258***	0.277***	0.281***
	(0.0078)	(0.0044)	(0.0065)	(0.0066)	(0.0100)
0.2 < land < 0.4 hectares	0.0415***	0.0341***	0.0288***	0.0230**	0.0327***
	(0.0086)	(0.0059)	(0.0072)	(0.0091)	(0.013)
0.4 < land < 2 hectares	0.0763***	0.0594***	0.0430***	0.0439***	0.0518**
	(0.015)	(0.011)	(0.013)	(0.017)	(0.021)
Land > 2 hectares	0.127***	0.126***	0.148***	0.147***	0.173***
	(0.018)	(0.022)	(0.027)	(0.016)	(0.030)
Household size	−0.118***	−0.140***	−0.162***	−0.184***	−0.206***
	(0.0045)	(0.0049)	(0.0048)	(0.0080)	(0.0086)
Household size square	0.00447***	0.00578***	0.00686***	0.00838***	0.00985***
	(0.00029)	(0.00029)	(0.00032)	(0.00062)	(0.00064)
Region controls					
North & East states					
Punjab	0.162***	0.109***	0.0714***	0.0571***	0.0433
	(0.013)	(0.021)	(0.015)	(0.022)	(0.037)
Delhi	0.184***	0.180***	0.135***	0.0970***	0.0604**
	(0.016)	(0.024)	(0.021)	(0.021)	(0.030)
Rajasthan	0.0802***	0.0535***	−0.00930	−0.0596***	−0.102***
	(0.019)	(0.012)	(0.015)	(0.012)	(0.036)
Uttar Pradesh	−0.0687***	−0.0729***	−0.103***	−0.130***	−0.149***
	(0.011)	(0.0096)	(0.0073)	(0.014)	(0.018)
Bihar	−0.171***	−0.197***	−0.257***	−0.281***	−0.330***
	(0.018)	(0.016)	(0.016)	(0.019)	(0.019)
Manipur	0.0381	−0.0538***	−0.126***	−0.195***	−0.265***
	(0.032)	(0.018)	(0.013)	(0.019)	(0.034)
Assam	−0.0702***	−0.0766***	−0.111***	−0.159***	−0.221***
	(0.025)	(0.019)	(0.014)	(0.012)	(0.021)
West Bengal	−0.0712***	−0.0617***	−0.106***	−0.132***	−0.160***
	(0.012)	(0.013)	(0.0079)	(0.0080)	(0.020)
Orissa	−0.310***	−0.328***	−0.324***	−0.343***	−0.352***
	(0.020)	(0.013)	(0.015)	(0.020)	(0.018)

(*continued*)

Table 3.2 (continued)

Independent Var.	q10	q25	q50	q75	q90
Central & West & South states					
Chhattisgarh	−0.163***	−0.202***	−0.254***	−0.231***	−0.243***
	(0.028)	(0.015)	(0.019)	(0.028)	(0.051)
Madhya Pradesh	−0.218***	−0.209***	−0.227***	−0.262***	−0.292***
	(0.023)	(0.019)	(0.012)	(0.018)	(0.028)
Gujarat	0.118***	0.124***	0.0822***	0.0212*	−0.0526***
	(0.022)	(0.017)	(0.011)	(0.013)	(0.014)
Maharashtra	−0.0118	−0.0174	−0.0281**	−0.0335*	−0.0493**
	(0.015)	(0.013)	(0.012)	(0.020)	(0.022)
Karnataka	−0.0671***	−0.0749***	−0.117***	−0.130***	−0.150***
	(0.018)	(0.015)	(0.012)	(0.014)	(0.026)
Kerala	0.0381	0.0830***	0.0664***	0.0711***	0.0981***
	(0.026)	(0.019)	(0.016)	(0.018)	(0.032)
Tamil Nadu	−0.143***	−0.126***	−0.154***	−0.148***	−0.146***
	(0.014)	(0.017)	(0.012)	(0.011)	(0.020)
Constant	5.726***	5.963***	6.181***	6.443***	6.807***
	(0.069)	(0.030)	(0.038)	(0.041)	(0.094)
Observations	26485	26485	26485	26485	26485

Notes: *Signifies $p < 0.05$; ** Signifies $p < 0.01$;*** Signifies $p < 0.001$. Standard errors are reported in parentheses. Dependent variable is log per-capita consumption expenditure. Base categories for occupation are salaried employee, for marital status is unmarried, for general/technical education is no general/technical education. Full set of state level regional dummies are also included in the regression with the excluded state being Andhra Pradesh

have lower welfare levels than self-employed households. This suggests the existence of a welfare hierarchy that is determined by the occupational choices of the members of the household.

These results suggest that employers are increasingly better off at higher quantiles than self- employed workers. Salaried employees who are in the middle of the distribution show the greatest difference from the self-employed individuals compared to those at the extreme quantiles. At higher quantiles, casual labourers are increasingly worse off than self-employed individuals are, and a similar phenomenon is observed for the unemployed.

The coefficients of control variables are in accordance with what might be expected. Households with older household heads are more likely to have higher consumption rates, and female-headed households are poorer across quantiles. Female-headed households are the worst off economically at the lowest quantile of the distribution. Households with a higher proportion of educated individuals have higher consumption rates, and the returns are increasing along the quantiles as well as along higher levels of education. The proportion of children less than 15 years old in the household has a significant negative effect at the lowest two quantiles, but this vanishes at higher quantiles. The proportion of females has an insignificant effect in the lower two quantiles but a significant positive effect at higher quantiles. Thus, at median, a 1% increase in the proportion of females increases the per-capita consumption by 4.4%, and at q(.9), by 9%. Consistent with earlier studies, the coefficients of the household size variables, demonstrate that households of larger size have a lower per-capita consumption expenditure. However, the household size squared term is positive and increases across quantiles, indicating that households of larger size become worse off along the quantiles, but at decreasing rates. Thus, a convex relationship exists between household size and welfare, with households in the middle of the distribution showing the greatest negative effect of size on per-capita consumption. This could be the result of higher economies of scale at the tails of the income distribution.

The quantile plots in Fig. 3.2 allow visualization of the estimated effects of the occupation variables on the per-capita consumption expenditure at different quantiles of the distribution. The *X*-axis shows the quantiles and the *Y*-axis shows the magnitude of the effect of the independent variables on the dependent variable. The dotted line shows the effect of the independent variable on the dependent variable if a simple ordinary least squares (OLS) regression is estimated. The curve shows the estimated effect of the independent variables on the per-capita consumption expenditure across different quantiles. The grey region around the curve shows the 95% confidence interval for the estimated effects. As the quantile plots in Fig. 3.2 show, the effect of occupation on the per-capita expenditure is non-linear and varies across quantiles.

As the first sub-plot shows, the effect of being employers on per-capita consumption expenditure increases across the quantiles, varying from 0.34 at the lowest quantile to 0.45 at the highest quantile. Although the

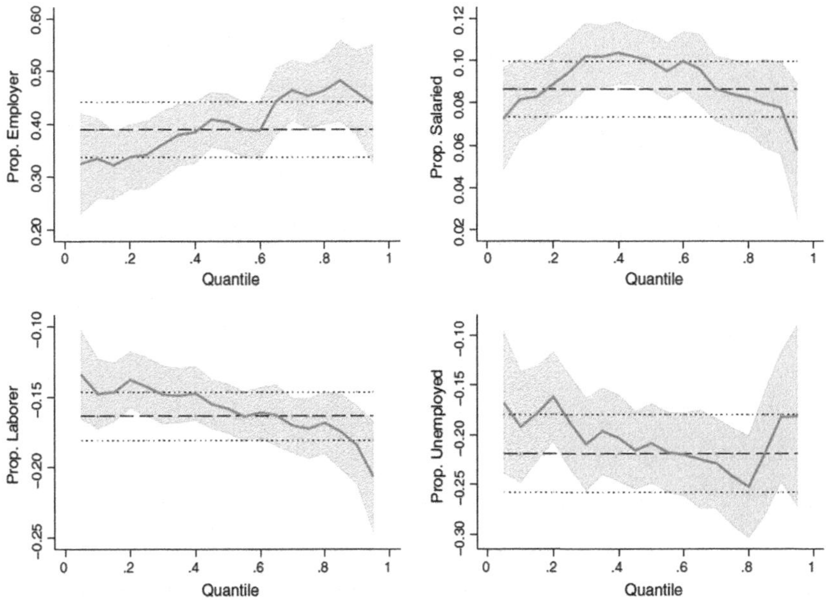

Fig. 3.2 Quantile plots. The graph shows the non-linear effects of the occupation variables, across different quantiles, on the per-capita consumption expenditure. The quantiles are on the *X*-axis, and the estimated effects of occupations on the per- capita consumption expenditure are on the *Y*-axis

effect is significantly positive throughout, the magnitude of the effect is much smaller at the lower quantiles than at the higher quantiles.

The second sub-plot shows that being salaried employees has a positive effect on per-capita consumption expenditure. However, the effect has an inverted U shape across quantiles. Similar non-linear effects are seen in the case of labourers and unemployed—the effects, however, are negative in both cases. Thus, estimating the mean effect of occupations on per-capita consumption expenditure in a simple OLS framework would not have captured these non-linear effects.

3.2.2 Analysis Restricted to Household Heads

One of the main limitations of the analysis of the household level occupation data is the simultaneous determination of the occupation of the household members leading to potential endogeneity of the occupation variables. The occupation of members of the household may not be independent of the occupation of the head of the household if there is intra-household dependence of occupational choice. In order to reduce the potential endogenous determination of the occupational choice of the household based on the occupational choice of the household head, we re-estimate the simultaneous quantile regressions for a restricted sample of households that have only the household head as the economically active individual in Table 3.3.

The base category for the occupation variables is 'salaried employee'. The estimation results are consistent with the estimations of the quantile regressions presented in Table 3.2. The results presented in Table 3.3 confirm the welfare hierarchy that the earlier regression suggested. Households headed by employers and salaried individuals have a higher per-capita consumption than households headed by self-employed individuals and casual labourers—after other factors that influence household welfare have been controlled. The magnitude of the coefficient of 'employer' suggests that households headed by entrepreneurs who employ others have the highest consumption levels. Relative to households headed by salaried employees, households headed by employers have consumption rates that 22.4% higher at the smallest quantile (q10), 25.8% higher at the median (q50), and 30.6% higher at the largest quantile (q90). Households headed by self-employed individuals have consumption rates that are 4.9% lower at the smallest quantile (q10), and 6.3% lower at the median (q50) when compared to salaried employees. The insignificant coefficient on the self-employed variable in the q90 column suggests that households headed by self- employed individuals and salaried employees have no significant difference in the consumption rates at the upper end of the distribution. The casual labourers are last in the hierarchy, and have consumption rates that are 20%–24.5% lower than self-employed individuals across the distribution. Thus, the results support the conjecture that

Table 3.3 Household heads, occupation, and consumption (*Estimates of simultaneous quantile regression*)

Independent Var.	q10	q25	q50	q75	q90
Occupation					
Self-employed	−0.0491***	−0.0579***	−0.0631***	−0.0564***	−0.0225
	(0.013)	(0.012)	(0.012)	(0.012)	(0.019)
Employer	0.224***	0.226***	0.258***	0.252***	0.306***
	(0.058)	(0.044)	(0.037)	(0.077)	(0.069)
Labourer	−0.228***	−0.229***	−0.246***	−0.225***	−0.203***
	(0.016)	(0.017)	(0.012)	(0.019)	(0.018)
Personal characteristics					
Age	0.0340***	0.0324***	0.0395***	0.0405***	0.0282***
	(0.0047)	(0.0039)	(0.0039)	(0.0043)	(0.0066)
Age square	−0.0371***	−0.0329***	−0.0409***	−0.0399***	−0.0240***
	(0.0061)	(0.0050)	(0.0048)	(0.0051)	(0.0083)
Female	−0.0144	−0.0296	−0.0653	0.0125	0.0811
	(0.035)	(0.031)	(0.043)	(0.041)	(0.060)
Married	−0.0301	−0.0312	−0.0321	−0.0658***	−0.0435
	(0.037)	(0.021)	(0.029)	(0.022)	(0.053)
Divorce/Widow	−0.212***	−0.233***	−0.176***	−0.220***	−0.184**
	(0.037)	(0.034)	(0.042)	(0.034)	(0.075)
General education					
Informal education	0.0479*	0.0390**	0.0219	0.0339*	0.0233
	(0.027)	(0.019)	(0.025)	(0.018)	(0.024)
Primary school	0.142***	0.146***	0.137***	0.172***	0.191***
	(0.018)	(0.013)	(0.018)	(0.018)	(0.016)
High school	0.235***	0.268***	0.292***	0.341***	0.361***
	(0.017)	(0.014)	(0.016)	(0.015)	(0.017)
University education	0.413***	0.483***	0.559***	0.640***	0.732***
	(0.025)	(0.015)	(0.019)	(0.023)	(0.022)
Technical degree or Diploma	0.170***	0.180***	0.169***	0.191***	0.235***
	(0.021)	(0.015)	(0.016)	(0.017)	(0.024)
Demographics	YES				
Household characteristics	YES				
Region controls	YES				
Sector controls	YES				

(*continued*)

Table 3.3 (continued)

Independent Var.	q10	q25	q50	q75	q90
Constant	5.773***	6.081***	6.237***	6.478***	6.923***
	(0.085)	(0.071)	(0.072)	(0.068)	(0.12)
Observations	13692	13692	13692	13692	13692

Notes: *Signifies $p < 0.05$; ** Signifies $p < 0.01$;*** Signifies $p < 0.001$. Standard errors are reported in parentheses. Dependent variable is log per-capita consumption expenditure. Base categories for occupation are salaried employee, for marital status is unmarried, for general/technical education is no general/ technical education. Full set of state level regional dummies are also included in the regression with the excluded state being Andhra Pradesh

relative returns to occupations differ across the welfare distribution and a comparison of returns at only the mean would not uncover these non-linear effects.

Table 3.4 suggests that at lower quantiles, informal education has a significantly positive effect on the per-capita consumption. The returns to primary school education increase along the quantiles. It is seen that at the smallest quantile [q(10)], primary schooling increases the per-capita consumption of the household by 14%. The coefficient, however, is higher at q(90), where it raises the per-capita consumption of household by 19%. A similar effect is observed for other education variables. If the household head has a high school education, per-capita consumption expenditure increases by 23% at the lowest quantile and 36% at the highest quantile. Similarly, if the household head has a university education, the per-capita consumption of the household increases by 41% at the lowest quantile and by 73% at the highest quantile. Thus, education has a positive effect on the per-capita consumption that increases as individuals move from the lower to higher quantiles. The returns to technical degree/diploma are also positive and increase as individuals shift from the lower to the higher quantiles.[7]

[7] As there are very few individuals with technical degrees or diplomas, we merge these into one variable.

Table 3.4 Household heads, occupation, and consumption (*Estimates of simultaneous quantile regression*)

Independent variable	ql0	q25	q50	q75	q90
Occupation					
Employer	0.224***	0.226***	0.258***	0.252***	0.306***
	(0.058)	(0.044)	(0.037)	(0.077)	(0.069)
Self-employed	−0.0491***	−0.0579***	−0.0631***	−0.0564***	−0.0225
	(0.013)	(0.012)	(0.012)	(0.012)	(0.019)
Labourer	−0.228***	−0.229***	−0.246***	−0.225***	−0.203***
	(0.016)	(0.017)	(0.012)	(0.019)	(0.018)
Personal characteristics					
Age	0.0340***	0.0324***	0.0395***	0.0405***	0.0282***
	(0.0047)	(0.0039)	(0.0039)	(0.0043)	(0.0066)
Age square	−0.0371***	−0.0329***	−0.0409***	−0.0399***	−0.0240***
	(0.0061)	(0.0050)	(0.0048)	(0.0051)	(0.0083)
Female	−0.0144	−0.0296	−0.0653	0.0125	0.0811
	(0.035)	(0.031)	(0.043)	(0.041)	(0.060)
Married	−0.0301	−0.0312	−0.0321	−0.0658***	−0.0435
	(0.037)	(0.021)	(0.029)	(0.022)	(0.053)
Divorce/Widow	−0.212***	−0.233***	−0.176***	−0.220***	−0.184**
	(0.037)	(0.034)	(0.042)	(0.034)	(0.075)
General education					
Informal education	0.0479*	0.0390**	0.0219	0.0339*	0.0233
	(0.027)	(0.019)	(0.025)	(0.018)	(0.024)
Primary school	0.142***	0.146***	0.137***	0.172***	0.191***
	(0.018)	(0.013)	(0.018)	(0.018)	(0.016)
High school	0.235***	0.268***	0.292***	0.341***	0.361***
	(0.017)	(0.014)	(0.016)	(0.015)	(0.017)
University education	0.413***	0.483***	0.559***	0.640***	0.732***
	(0.025)	(0.015)	(0.019)	(0.023)	(0.022)
Technical Degree or Diploma	0.170***	0.180***	0.169***	0.191***	0.235***
	(0.021)	(0.015)	(0.016)	(0.017)	(0.024)
Demographics	Yes				
Household characteristics	Yes				
Region controls	Yes				
Sector controls	Yes				

(*continued*)

Table 3.4 (continued)

Independent variable	q10	q25	q50	q75	q90
Constant	5.773***	6.081***	6.237***	6.478***	6.923***
	(0.085)	(0.071)	(0.072)	(0.068)	(0.12)
Observations	13,692	13,692	13,692	13,692	13,692

*$p < 0.05$, ** $p < 0.01$, ***$p < 0.001$ Standard errors are reported in parentheses
The dependent variable is log per-capita consumption expenditure. The base category for occupation is the salaried employee; for marital status, unmarried; for general/technical education, no general/technical education. A full set of state level regional dummies is also included in the regression, with the excluded state being Andhra Pradesh

3.2.3 Occupation and Poverty

Now, we predict per-capita consumption of individuals following the quantile regression estimations to examine the relative poverty levels across different occupational groups.[8] The cumulative distribution plots of occupation-wise predicted values are shown in Fig. 3.3. The per-capita expenditure is on the *X*-axis and the cumulative probability is on the *Y*-axis. At any point *x* on the *X*-axis, the cumulative distribution function of a particular occupational category would give the proportion of individuals in that occupational category whose consumption is below *x*. It can be seen that in all the sub-plots of Fig. 3.3, at any given point *x* on the *X*-axis, the proportion of employers whose per-capita consumption expenditure is below *x* is lower than the proportion of salaried employees whose per-capita expenditure is below *x*. An analogous argument implies that the proportion of salaried employees whose per-capita consumption expenditure is below *x* is lower than the proportion of self- employed individuals or casual labourers whose per- capita consumption expenditure is below *x*. The plots show that the cumulative distribution function of employers stochastically dominates the distributions of other occupational categories. Since *x* is any point on the *X*-axis, the figure does away

[8] The log-inverse transformation of the predicted values gives the value of the normalized per-capita consumption expenditure. These transformed values are used in the poverty analysis.

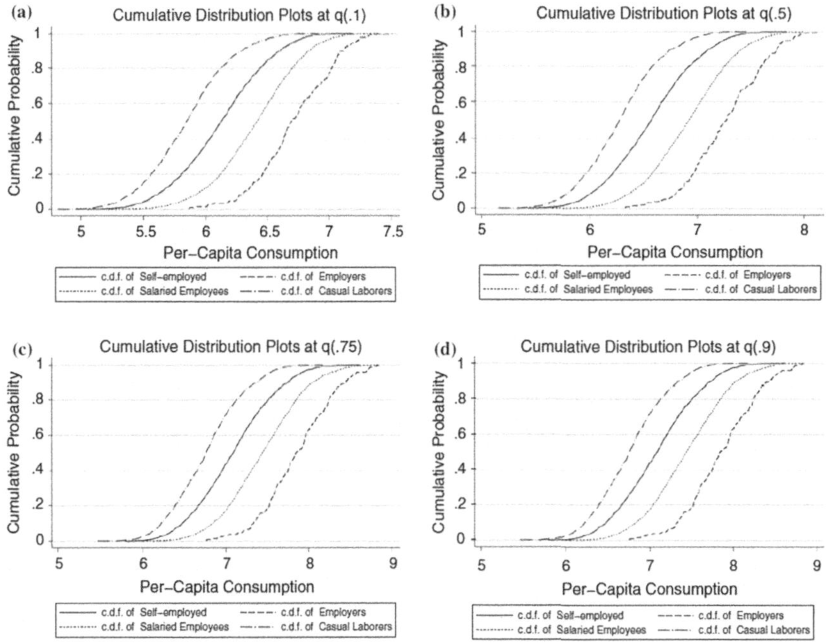

Fig. 3.3 Occupation and poverty plots (normalized)

with the necessity of having a fixed poverty line to examine the relative poverty in different occupational groups.

A simple mathematical formulation of the above arguments is as follows. Let the cumulative distribution functions of the four occupational categories be given by functions F_{emp} for employers, F_{sal} for salaried employees, F_{self} for self-employed individuals, and F_{lab} for labourers. At any given point *x* on the *X*-axis, the plots show that $F_{emp}(x) > F_{sal}(x) > F_{self}(x) > F_{lab}(x)$. Thus, the employers group would have the least proportion of people under the poverty line, if the poverty line is at *x*.

The plot clarifies the status of the self-employed; they appear to be sandwiched between the salaried employees and the casual labourers. A direct implication of this observation is that, conditional on other characteristics, individuals in the informal sector, primarily comprising the self-employed and the casual labourers, have lower returns to their occupations. Furthermore, if the dataset is split into formal and informal sectors, with labourers and self-employed in the informal sector and salaried employees and employers in the formal sector, the plots suggest that in both sectors, entrepreneurship in the form of employers in the formal sector and self-employed in the informal sector entails higher relative consumption.

Consistent with above, when occupational choice is estimated as a determinant of poverty of households using a probit model using a relative measure of poverty given by half of the median per-capita consumption of all the households, the results suggest that households headed by employers, self-employed, and salaried employees are less likely to be under the poverty line unlike households headed by casual labourers.[9]

3.3 Conclusions

Using simultaneous quantile regressions, we find that employers, those entrepreneurs who also hire others, have the highest returns in terms of consumption, while the self-employed individuals have slightly lower returns than salaried employees. The results demonstrate that the relative returns to occupations differ at different points of the welfare distribution. For instance, although the consumption rates of self-employed household heads is significantly lower at many points of the distribution relative to the salaried household heads, there is no significant difference at the highest quantile. A comparison of returns at the mean alone would not have uncovered these non-linear effects. When compared to casual labourers, self-employed individuals are more likely to escape poverty while entrepreneurs who are employers have the highest returns of all occupational groups.

[9] Using an alternate poverty line based on the number of adults has not significantly altered the main inferences. These results are not presented here but are available upon request.

References

Blau, D. M. (1987). A time series analysis of self-employment in United States. *Journal of Political Economy, 95*(3), 445–467.

Browning, M., & Lusardi, A. (1996). Household saving: Micro theories and micro facts. *Journal of Economic Literature, 34*(4), 1797–1855.

Cunningham, W. V., & Maloney, W. F. (2001). Heterogeneity in the Mexican micro-enterprise sector. *Economic Development and Cultural Change, 50*, 131–156.

Deaton, A. S., & Muellbauer, J. (1980). *Economics and consumer behavior.* Cambridge: Cambridge University Press.

Deaton, A. S., & Muellbauer, J. (1986). On measuring child costs: With applications to poor countries. *The Journal of Political Economy, 94*(4), 720–744.

Fields, G. S. (2005). *A guide to multisector labor market models.* Social protection discussion paper series No. 0505. Washington D.C.: World Bank.

Gindling, T. H. (1991). Labor market segmentation and the determination of wages in the public, private-formal and informal sectors in San-Jose, Costa-Rica. *Economic Development and Cultural Change, 39*, 585–605.

Günther, I., & Launov, A. (2006). *Competitive and segmented informal labor markets.* IZA discussion papers 2349. Bonn: Institute for the Study of Labor (IZA).

Hamilton, B. H. (2000). Does entrepreneurship pay? An empirical analysis of the returns of self-employment. *Journal of Political Economy, 108*(3), 604–631.

Koenker, R., & Hallock, H. F. (2001). Quantile regression: An introduction. *Journal of Economic Perspectives, 15*(4), 143–156.

Lazear, E. P., & Michael, R. T. (1980). Family size and the distribution of real per capita income. *American Economic Review, 70*(1), 91–107.

Magnac, T. (1991). Segmented or competitive labor markets. *Econometrica, 59*, 165–187.

Maloney, W. F. (2004). Informality revisited. *World Development, 32*(7), 1159–1178.

Muellbauer, J. (1974). Household composition, engel curves and welfare comparisons between households. *European Economic Review, 5*, 103–122.

Parker, S. C. (1996). A time series model of self-employment under uncertainty. *Economica, 63*, 469–475.

Parker, S. C. (2018). *The economics of entrepreneurship.* Cambridge University Press.

Pratap, S., & Quintin, E. (2006). Are labor markets segmented in developing countries? A semiparametric approach. *European Economic Review, 50*, 1817–1841.

Rees, H., & Shaw, A. (1986). An empirical analysis of self- employment in UK. *Journal of Applied Econometrics, 1*, 95–108.

Rosen, S. (1981). The economics of superstars. *American Economic Review, 71*(5), 845–858.

Wodon, Q. T. (2000). Microdeterminants of consumption, poverty, growth, and inequality in Bangladesh. *Applied Economics, 32*(10), 1337–1352.

4

Size of New Start-ups Across Space

4.1 Firm Start-Up Size and Location

As Geroski (1995) and Caves (1998) summarize an extensive empirical literature, the likelihood of survival for new entrants is low, and those that do survive grow at a higher rate than the incumbents. Firms with a larger start-up size have a higher likelihood of survival (Dunne, Roberts, & Samuelson, 1989; Mata, Portugal, & Guimaraes, 1995). Thus, the size of a new firm at start-up has a significant impact on its post-entry performance and survival.

The empirical studies on the determinants of firm start-up size primarily examine the role played by industry characteristics such as the minimum efficient scale (MES) of the industry, industry growth, effects of operation at sub-optimal scale (defined as the proportion of those employed in firms that are operating at sub-optimal scale), impact of market size (Mata & Machado, 1996; Mata, 1996; Görg & Ruane, 2000; Görg & Strobl, 2002) and firm specific characteristics such as human capital of founders and credit constraints (Astebro & Bernhardt, 2005; Colombo, Delmastro, & Grilli, 2004; Colombo & Grilli, 2005).

These studies suggest that the size of new firms tends to be greater in industries with a higher minimum efficient scale (MES), greater turbulence, and in industries where few sub-optimal firms operate (Mata,

J. P. Tamvada, *Microentrepreneurship in a Developing Country*,
https://doi.org/10.1007/978-3-030-68628-4_4

1996). As Mata and Machado (1996, p. 1321) note, "entry on a relatively large scale in each industry is much more sensitive to the minimum efficient scale and to the extent of firm turnover in the industry than entry in small scale. Put differently, it seems that small new firms appear everywhere, while relatively large ones only appear where economies of scale make it crucial, or where sunk costs are low, therefore leading to low losses in case of failure."[1]

The start-up size is also influenced by characteristics specific to the firm. In particular, as the age and education of the founder increase, firm start-up size has been found to increase along with it. Professional knowledge about the particular industry along with managerial and entrepreneurial experience have been found to have a greater positive impact than education and working experience on the size of new firms (Colombo et al., 2004).[2] Similarly, Astebro and Bernhardt (2005) find that the entrepreneurial human capital of founders co-determines their household wealth as well as their firm's start-up capital.

There are compelling reasons already established in the economics literature to suggest that start-up size may not be independent of the geographic location. A new literature has emerged suggesting that knowledge, competence, and know-how spills over from the firm producing it to a different, third-party firm (Griliches, 1992). This view is supported by theoretical models which have focused on the role that spillovers of knowledge play in generating increasing returns and ultimately economic growth (Romer, 1986, 1990, 1994; Krugman, 1991a, 1991b). An important theoretical development is that geography may provide a relevant unit of observation within which knowledge spillovers occur. The theory of localization suggests that because geographic proximity is needed to transmit knowledge and especially tacit knowledge, knowledge spillovers

[1] A study on Irish firms shows comparable results, but finds a negative effect of industry size and positive effect of industry growth on start-up size (Görg & Ruane, 2000). Nurmi (2006) studies sectoral differences in size of firm start-ups in Finland and finds that results for manufacturing and service sectors are very similar. Görg and Strobl (2002) find that the presence of multinationals in an industry negatively effects the size of domestic Irish entrants. Mata and Machado (1996) analyse a sample of 1079 new firms from Portugal. In their sample, not more than 25% have greater than the average size of 17 employees, and 50% of the firms employ less than 10 people.

[2] Colombo et al. (2004) investigate start-up size of 391 technology-based young Italian firms in both manufacturing and services.

tend to be localized within a geographic region. The importance of geographic proximity for spillovers has been supported in a wave of recent empirical studies by (Jaffe, 1989; Jaffe, Trajtenberg, & Henderson, 1993; Audretsch & Feldman, 1996; Audretsch & Stephan, 1996). Such external knowledge resources should impact the firm start-up size by enabling the new firm to attract more early stage resources in order to start up at a greater scale, that is, size. Thus, such spatially constrained externalities will have an impact on the size of new firm start-ups, reflecting the availability of knowledge external to the start-up.

Furthermore, spatial location may have an impact on the size of new firm start-ups if the level of financial development significantly differs across regions.[3] Financial constraints have an impact on the size of new firm start-ups. For example, Colombo and Grilli (2005) find that firms receiving external private equity financing have a larger size at start-up. Cabral and Mata (2003) suggest that the firm size distribution evolves from a right skewed distribution to a less skewed distribution over time as financial constraints become less binding over time.[4] At the level of regions, financial development influences firm size distribution (Beck, Demirguc-Kunt, Laeven, & Levine, 2006), and is likely to impact the size at start-up.

As regional specific variables such as human capital, knowledge stock, unemployment, sector specialization, and income and population growth explain the variation in the new firm formation rates across regions (Acs & Armington, 2006), spatial location may also have an impact on the size of new firm start-ups through these economic channels. Here we go beyond firm entry rates, to explicitly examine if the size of new firm start-ups systematically varies across space.

[3] For example, Burgess and Pande (2005) show that financial development differs across Indian regions has an impact on poverty.

[4] However, by using measures of financial constraints from firm level data, Angelini and Generale (2008) find that although the FSD of constrained firms is more right skewed, the FSD of unconstrained firms is indistinguishable from the FSD of all firms. Further, they find that financial constraints are more relevant in developing countries in explaining the FSD.

4.2 Firm Start-Up Size Across Space in India

The main source of data for linking the geographic location of the firm with the start-up size is from the Ministry of Small Scale Industries in India. We use firm level data from the third census of registered small scale firms. This census was conducted in 2001. We consider manufacturing firms that have started producing in 1998, 1999, or 2000 as new start-ups for the analysis following Audretsch, Keilbach, and Lehman (2006), who consider the three year period, as firm start-ups are subject to a very high degree of stochastic disturbance if only a very short period is considered. This rich dataset of entrants consists of 149,708 firms. Each new firm was asked a series of questions concerning the set of initial conditions under which it was founded (such as the original value of its plant and machinery, its year of initial production, the sector, the source of its technical knowledge, its spatial location). As the dataset consists solely of small firms, we do not have information about large entrants. This limitation of the dataset, however, does not pose serious problems for testing our hypothesis, since the theory of firm size distribution suggests that the majority of entrants are small and numerous. Furthermore, if few large entrants are also present in the dataset, they would at best be outliers and introduce heterogeneity.[5]

As the descriptive statistics in Table 4.1 suggest 88.5% of the sample consists of firms that were started by proprietors. 6.8% of the firms are owned by two or more partners and are referred to as partnerships. Firms having other ownership structures such as co-operatives account for 4.7% of the sample. 15.8% of the firms are managed by women. 73.8% are small scale industrial units. Thus, 26.2% of the firms are small scale business enterprises, primarily consisting of repairing, servicing, and maintenance units. More than 14% of the firms have reported that they have technical knowledge. While only 0.94% of the firms in the sample reported having obtained knowledge from sources outside India, as many as 6.6% have their technical knowledge from other firms and 6.67%

[5] This is one of the main reasons for the studies on the start-up size to use quantile regressions (Mata & Machado, 1996; Görg & Ruane, 2000; Colombo et al., 2004). Also, there is compelling evidence that entry takes place in the form of new small firms (Audretsch, 1995; Dunne et al., 1989).

Table 4.1 Characteristics of start-ups (descriptives)

Log (employment)	1.0768
Std. Dev.	(*0.8382*)
Log (Value of plant and machinery)	10.5329
Std. Dev.	(*1.9202*)
Proprietary	0.8850
Partnership	0.0678
Other ownership	0.0472
Managed by woman	0.1581
Small scale industry (SSI)	0.7382
Small scale business enterprise (SSBE)	0.2618
Tech knowledge (foreign)	0.0097
Tech knowledge (firm)	0.0659
Tech knowledge (university)	0.0667
Food products	0.1922
Tobacco	0.0013
Textiles	0.0490
Apparels	0.2090
Leather	0.0226
Wood	0.0391
Paper	0.0112
Printing	0.0382
Coke	0.0046
Chemicals	0.0368
Rubber	0.0432
Minerals	0.0651
Basic metals	0.0168
Fabricated metals	0.1167
Machinery	0.0290
Computing machinery	0.0021
Electric machinery	0.0233
Communication equipment	0.0051
Precision instruments	0.0036
Motor vehicles	0.0062
Transport equipment	0.0028
Furniture	0.0814
Recycling	0.0004

from universities. 20.9% of the firms are in the industrial sub-sector of apparels manufacture and 19.2% are firms dealing with food products. With 11.67% of all the firms, the next largest group comprises of firms in the industrial sub-sector of fabricated metals.

Using the Bayesian methodology described in Chap. 2, firm and industry characteristics as well as spatial location are introduced simultaneously in the following geoadditive regression framework.[6]

$$\eta = \gamma_{const} + \gamma_{Proprietary\,Ownership} + \gamma_{Woman} + \gamma_{Technical\,Knowledge} + \gamma_{Urban} + \gamma_{Industrial\,Sector} + f_{spatial}(district) + f_{random}(district)$$

The *dependent variable* is the start-up size of new firms. Two different measures of the dependent variable are used for the empirical analysis. In the first model, the start-up size is given by the initial value of fixed assets. In the second model, it is given by the initial employment of the firm.

Figure 4.1 shows that the size of the new firm start-ups, measured by initial value of fixed assets, systematically varies across space even after controlling for the firm and industry characteristics.

As the structured spatial effects in Fig. 4.1a show, while districts of Maharashtra and Andhra Pradesh form a belt exhibiting a significantly larger size new firm start-ups, the districts of Uttar Pradesh, Madhya Pradesh, and Bihar, form a belt with significantly smaller new firm start-up size.[7] As the 95% and 80% confidence maps in Figs. 4.1c, d show, the effects are mostly statistically significant.[8]

The estimated effects of the variables in the parametric part of the geoadditive model are broadly consistent with the existing literature. As the results in Table 4.2 show, ownership type has a significant influence on

---

[6] The model is estimated using the Bayesian software BayesX. The structured spatial effects are estimated based on Markov random field priors and random spatial effects are estimated with Gaussian priors. The variance components in all the cases are estimated based on inverse gamma priors with hyperparameters a = 0.001 and b = 0.001. The number of iterations is set to 120000 with burnin parameter set to 20000 and the thinning parameter set to 100. The autocorrelation files and the sampling paths show that the MCMC algorithm has converged. These plots are available from the author.

[7] As discussed in the method section, the total spatial effect is split into the structured spatial component and an unstructured local random component. The unstructured random component corresponds to the random error component of the geoadditive model. The map of the estimated unstructured random component in Fig. 4.1b shows that the local spatial effects are smaller than the structured spatial effects suggesting that the effect of geographic space is continuous and not purely random.

[8] Because industry effects are controlled in the estimation, these results cannot be attributed to the effect of spatial distribution of labour-intensive industries.

(a)

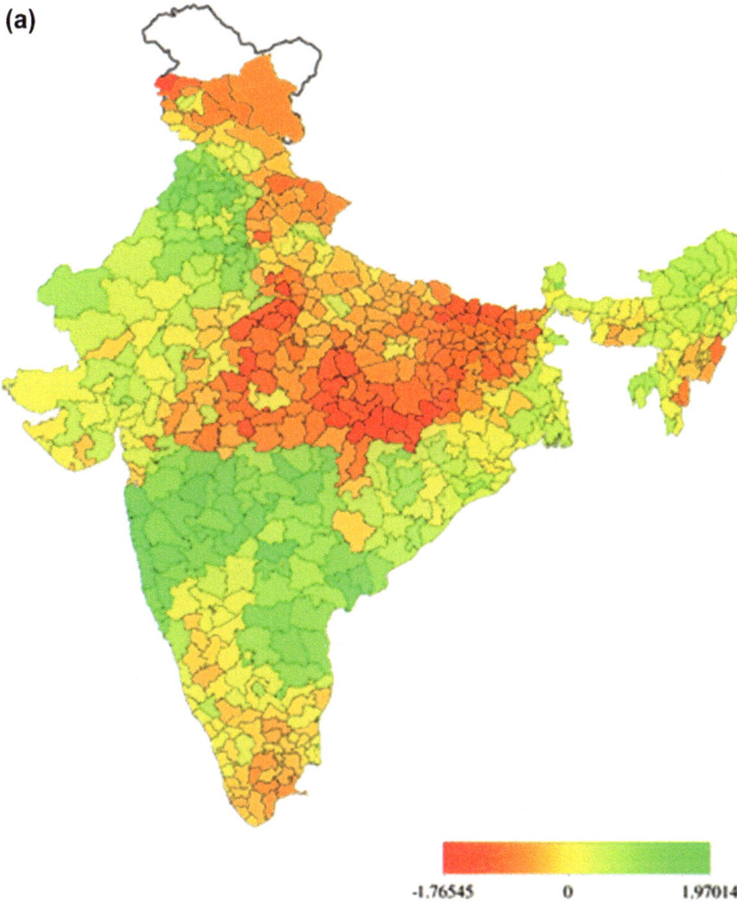

Fig. 4.1 Spatial effects in model I. (a) Structured non-linear effect of 'District'. Shown are the posterior means. (b) Unstructured random effect of 'District'. Shown are the posterior means. (c) Non-linear effect of 'District'. Posterior probabilities for a nominal level of 95%. Black denotes regions with strictly negative credible intervals, and white denotes regions with strictly positive credible intervals.

The white areas in Jammu and Kashmir are regions not included in the estimations. (d) Non-linear effect of 'District'. Posterior probabilities for a nominal level of 80%. Black denotes regions with strictly negative credible intervals, and white denotes regions with strictly positive credible intervals. The white areas in Jammu and Kashmir are regions not included in the estimations. (Notes: The maps are plotted for areas that are statistically estimable and do not show political boundaries of India)

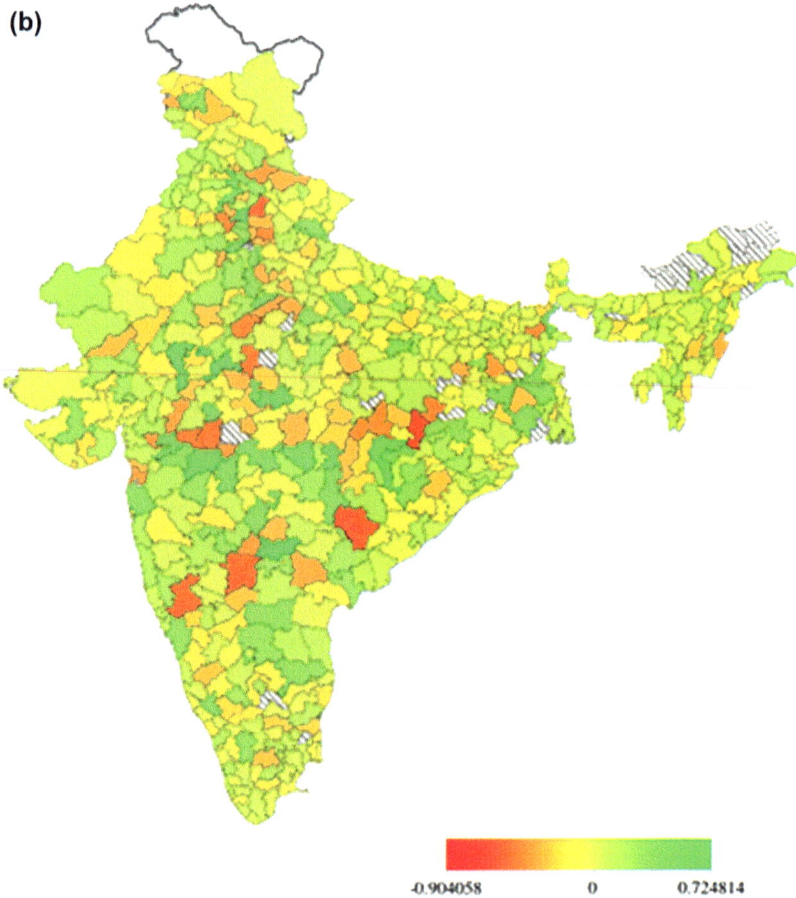

Fig. 4.1 (continued)

(c)

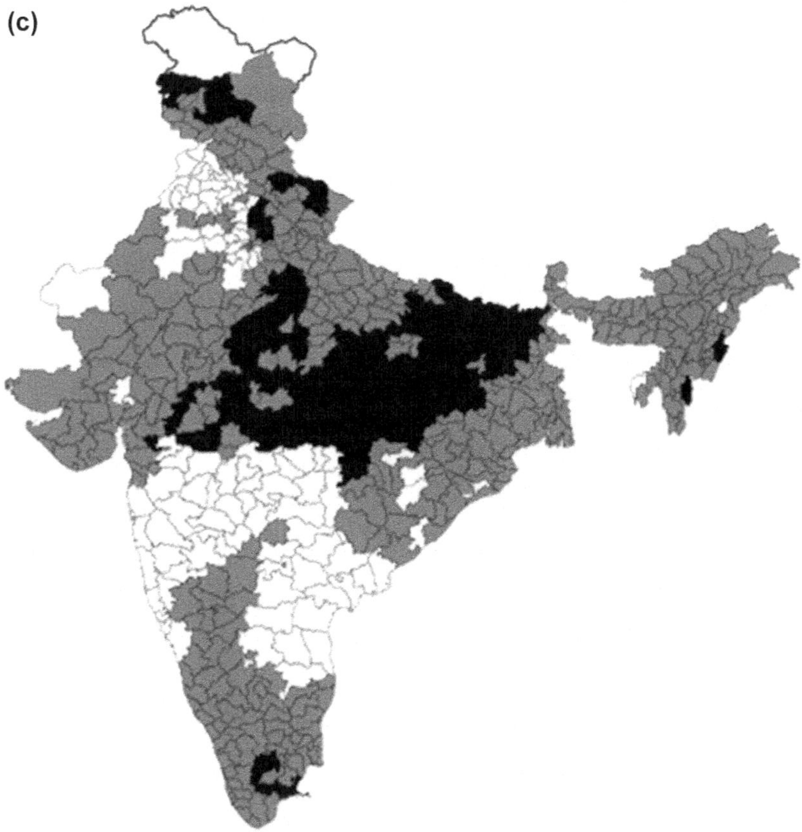

Fig. 4.1 (continued)

(d)

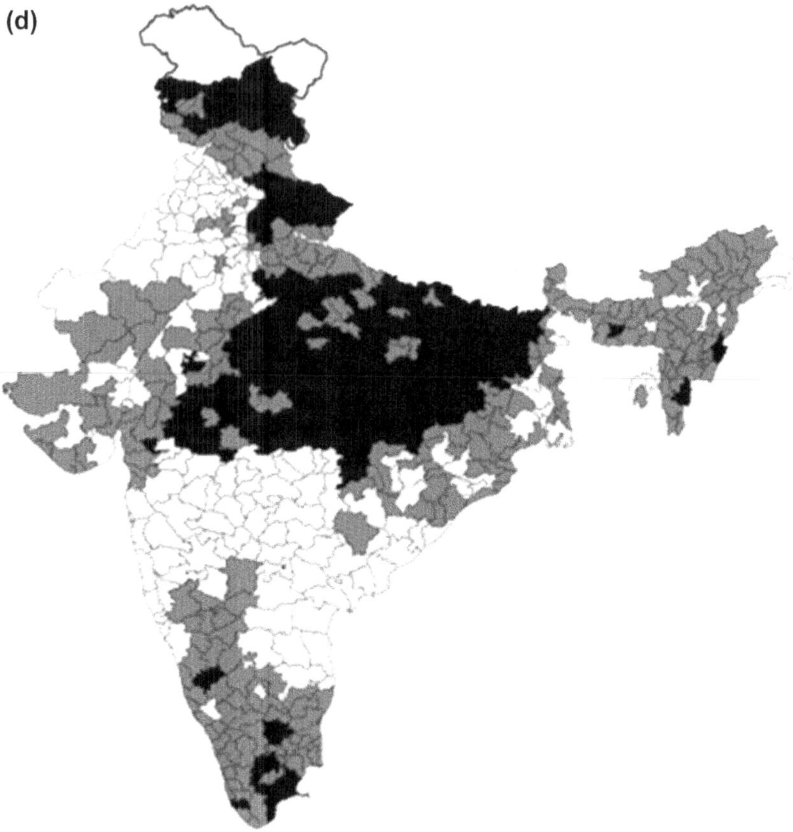

Fig. 4.1 (continued)

Table 4.2 Determinants of start-up size (Model I) (*Initial value of fixed assets*)

Variable	Mean	Std. Dev.	2.5%-Qt.	97.5%-Qt.
Ownership structure				
Proprietary	−1.408	0.012	−1.433	−1.384
Woman	−0.547	0.011	−0.567	−0.526
Technical knowledge				
Tech knowledge (Foreign)	0.444	0.038	0.373	0.516
Tech knowledge (Firm)	0.213	0.016	0.183	0.244
Tech knowledge (University)	0.289	0.016	0.258	0.319
Firm type				
SSI	0.508	0.011	0.486	0.529
Urban	0.194	0.008	0.177	0.211
Industries				
Tobacco	−0.986	0.102	−1.180	−0.786
Textiles	−0.465	0.021	−0.506	−0.424
Apparels	−1.067	0.014	−1.094	−1.040
Leather	−1.439	0.026	−1.492	−1.388
Wood	−1.041	0.019	−1.079	−1.001
Paper	0.048	0.037	−0.023	0.121
Printing	0.008	0.021	−0.034	0.048
Coke	0.587	0.057	0.478	0.699
Chemicals	−0.349	0.021	−0.389	−0.306
Rubber	0.133	0.020	0.095	0.171
Minerals	−0.114	0.017	−0.147	−0.082
Basic metals	0.078	0.029	0.019	0.131
Fabricated metals	−0.378	0.014	−0.404	−0.350
Machinery	−0.264	0.023	−0.308	−0.220
Computing machinery	−0.609	0.076	−0.758	−0.467
Electric machinery	−0.724	0.025	−0.772	−0.671
Communication equipment	−0.722	0.053	−0.820	−0.617
Precision instruments	−0.282	0.060	−0.403	−0.161
Motor vehicles	0.243	0.047	0.153	0.337
Transport equipment	−0.439	0.068	−0.572	−0.304
Furniture	−1.040	0.015	−1.069	−1.011
Recycling	0.069	0.177	−0.276	0.438
Year controls				
Year 1999	0.064	0.008	0.048	0.080
Year 2000	0.086	0.009	0.068	0.104
Constant	11.867	0.027	11.813	11.921
Observations	146519			

Notes: Dependent variable is log of initial value of fixed assets of the firm the size of new firm start-ups.[9] New-firm start-ups by proprietary owners and female entrepreneurs have a smaller size at start-up. The results suggest that entrepreneurs with technical know-how start-up with a larger firm size. Technical knowledge from abroad increases the size of new firm start-ups by 44%, technical knowledge from other firms increases it by 21%, and technical knowledge from universities increases it by 29%. Thus, firms that have technical knowledge at the start-up phase tend to have a larger start-up size than firms that do not have any technical knowledge.

The estimated spatial effects in the second specification-with initial employment as the dependent variable-demonstrate a similar spatial pattern as in the first model. As the maps plotted in Fig. 4.2 show, the new firm start-ups in northern states of Uttaranchal, Uttar Pradesh, Bihar, Madhya Pradesh, and Rajasthan as well as some districts of the southern states of Kerala, Karnataka, and Tamil Nadu are likely to be smaller. In contrast, new firm start-ups in the states of Maharashtra, Andhra Pradesh, West Bengal, Punjab, and the North eastern states have a larger size.

Table 4.3 shows that the estimated effects of variables in the parametric part of the geoadditive model are robust to this alternate specification with the firm start-up size measured by the initial employment. Proprietary owners and women entrepreneurs start up with a smaller firm size. Entrepreneurs with technical knowledge start up with a larger firm size. New firms started by entrepreneurs in urban locations have a larger size.

The estimation results for both models demonstrate that firm and industry effects do not completely explain the size of new firm start-ups; the size of new firm start-ups systematically varies over space even after accounting for firm and industry effects. Thus, spatial location has an impact on the size of new firm start-ups. The estimated spatial effects clearly suggest a north-south divide in the size of new firm start-ups. New firms in the northern regions have a significantly smaller size when compared to the new firm start-ups in the southern regions, *ceteris paribus*.

The maps show that spatial effects are continuous over space-contiguous districts in the north and have a significantly negative effect (these districts are coloured either red or black in the maps) and contiguous

[9] The effect of firm ownership structure on start-up size is estimated, as firms that have proprietary ownership structure are likely to be small compared to those that have partnership or co-operative ownership structures.

(a)

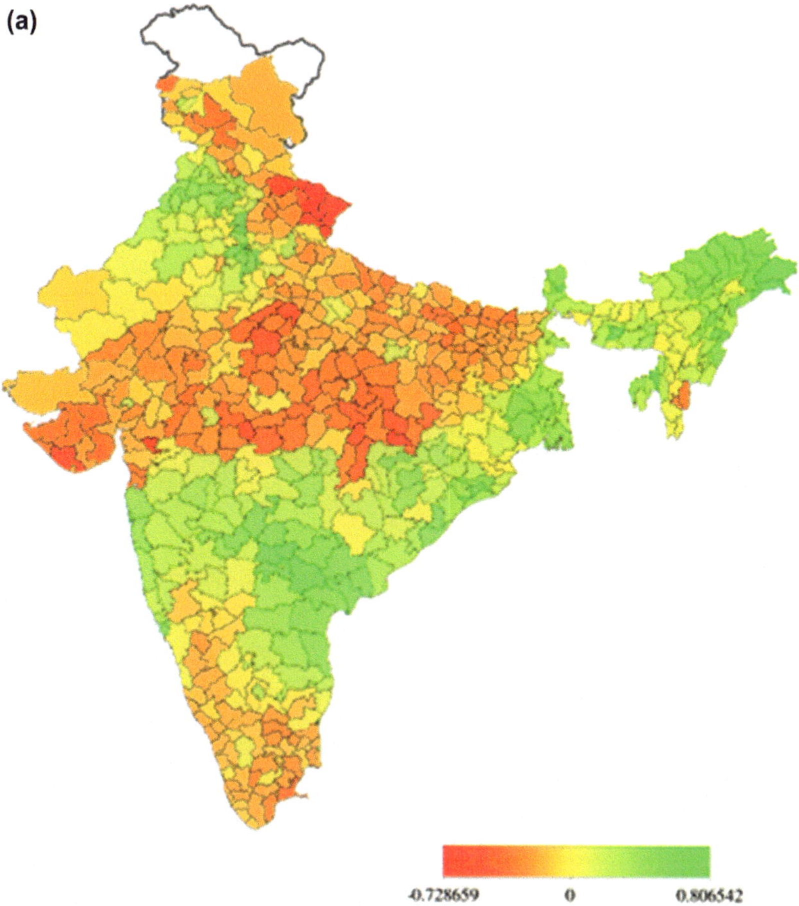

Fig. 4.2 Spatial effects in model II. (a) Structured non-linear effect of 'District'. Shown are the posterior means. (b) Unstructured random effect of 'District'. Shown are the posterior means. (c) Non-linear effect of 'District'. Posterior probabilities for a nominal level of 95%. Black denotes regions with strictly negative credible intervals, and white denotes regions with strictly positive credible intervals.

The white areas in Jammu and Kashmir are regions not included in the estimations. (d) Non-linear effect of 'District'. Posterior probabilities for a nominal level of 80%. Black denotes regions with strictly negative credible intervals, and white denotes regions with strictly positive credible intervals. The white areas in Jammu and Kashmir are regions not included in the estimations. (Notes: The maps are plotted for areas that are statistically estimable and do not show political boundaries of India)

(b)

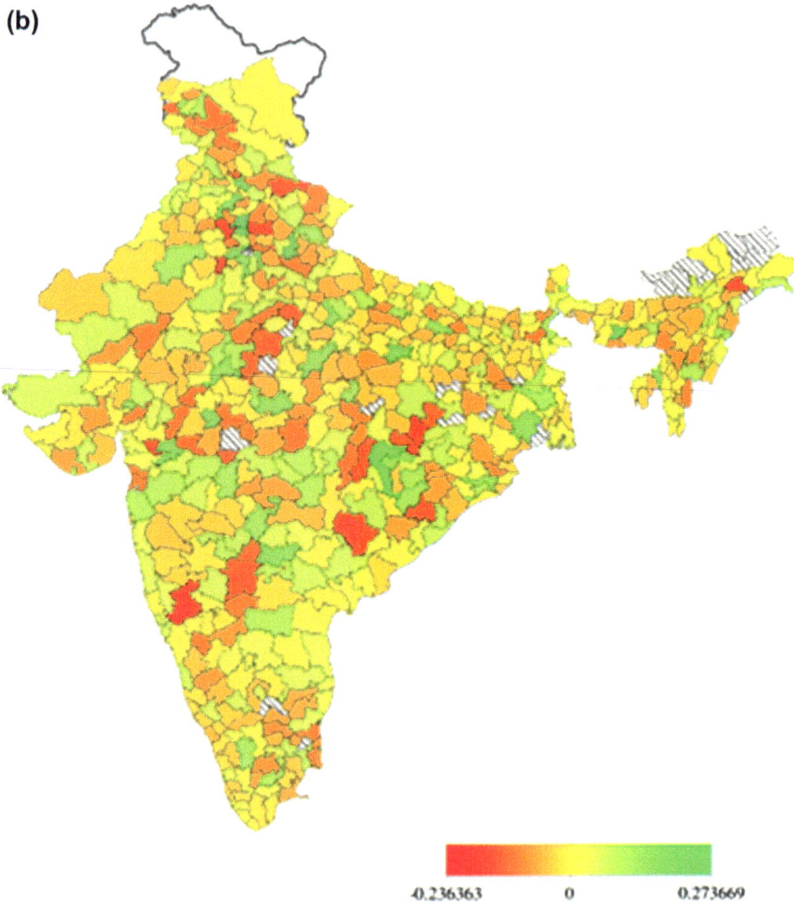

Fig. 4.2 (continued)

(c)

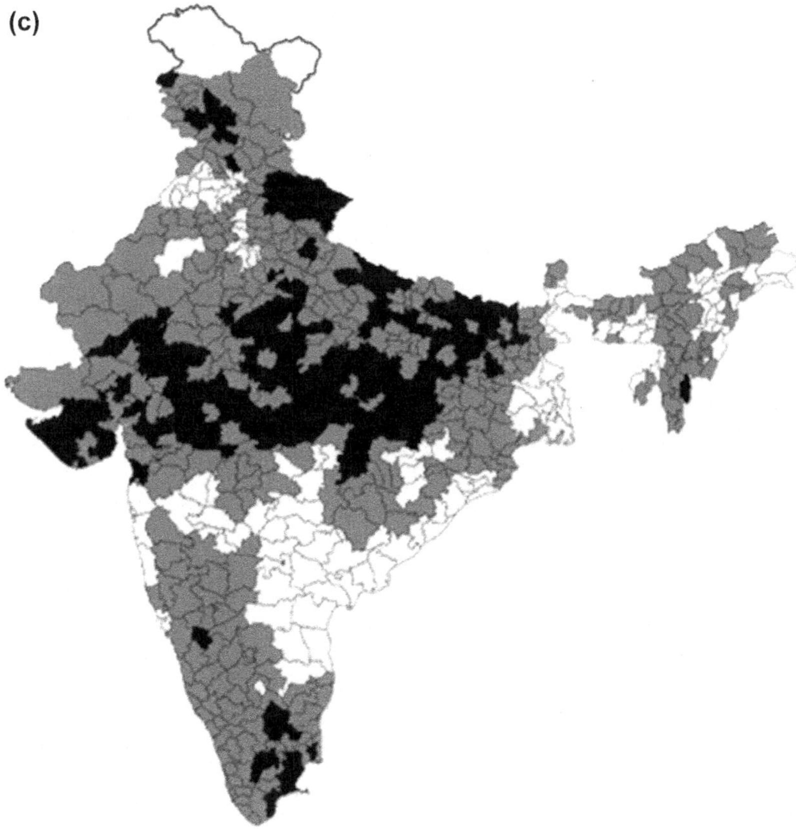

Fig. 4.2 (continued)

(d)

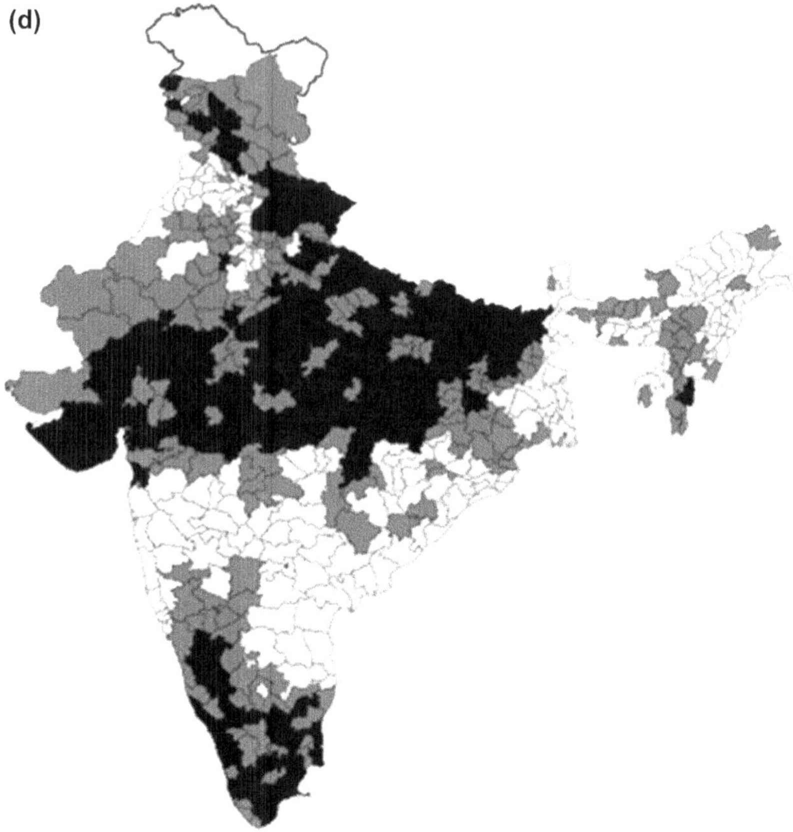

Fig. 4.2 (continued)

Table 4.3 Determinants of start-up size (Model II) (*Determinants of initial employment*)

Variable	Mean	Std. Dev.	2.5%-Qt.	97.5%-Qt.
Ownership structure				
Proprietary	−0.666	0.006	−0.677	−0.655
Woman	−0.180	0.005	−0.190	−0.171
Technical knowledge				
Tech knowledge (foreign)	0.152	0.017	0.119	0.185
Tech knowledge (firm)	0.078	0.007	0.063	0.091
Tech knowledge (university)	0.083	0.007	0.069	0.098
Firm type				
SSI	0.408	0.005	0.398	0.418
Urban	0.075	0.004	0.068	0.082
Industries				
Tobacco	0.309	0.047	0.222	0.401
Textiles	0.329	0.009	0.312	0.347
Apparels	0.014	0.006	0.001	0.026
Leather	−0.122	0.012	−0.145	−0.098
Wood	0.012	0.009	−0.007	0.029
Paper	0.273	0.016	0.239	0.307
Printing	−0.013	0.010	−0.031	0.006
Coke	0.498	0.025	0.449	0.547
Chemicals	0.264	0.010	0.244	0.282
Rubber	0.168	0.009	0.150	0.185
Minerals	0.530	0.008	0.515	0.545
Basic metals	0.326	0.014	0.298	0.355
Fabricated metals	0.038	0.007	0.026	0.051
Machinery	0.099	0.011	0.078	0.119
Computing machinery	−0.152	0.036	−0.220	−0.084
Electric machinery	−0.046	0.012	−0.069	−0.023
Communication equipment	−0.010	0.023	−0.052	0.036
Precision instruments	0.113	0.029	0.057	0.174
Motor vehicles	0.377	0.021	0.335	0.419
Transport equipment	0.169	0.032	0.106	0.231
Furniture	−0.041	0.007	−0.056	−0.028
Recycling	0.344	0.082	0.183	0.498
Year controls				
Year 1999	0.016	0.004	0.009	0.024
Year 2000	0.025	0.004	0.017	0.034
Constant	1.323	0.011	1.302	1.343
Observations	149709			

Notes: Dependent variable is log of initial employment of the firm districts in the south have a significantly positive effect (these districts are coloured either green or white in the maps).

We now investigate the factors influencing these spatial patterns. In particular, it may be conjectured that factors such as economic development, financial development, literacy, and unemployment are shaping these spatial patterns. There is overwhelming evidence that financial development has an important economic role (see Levine, 1997, for a survey). At the level of the firm, Cabral and Mata (2003) find that the firm size distribution is right skewed for start-ups but evolves over time to a less skewed distribution as financial constraints become less binding over time. Thus, variation in financial development across space may have an influence on these estimated spatial patterns.[10] Lucas (1978) argues that the average firm size increases with economic development. For these reasons, regional variations in the level of economic development may play a significant role in shaping these spatial patterns.

High level of unemployment may compel people into self-employment and make them start small micro-enterprises. Regions with higher levels of literacy may give birth to firms with larger size at start-up as education is likely to improve organizational skills of individuals. Agglomeration is likely to have an impact on the size of new firm start-ups. While a high level of agglomeration may give rise to externalities that have a positive effect on the size of new firms in the region, it may also reflect the presence of number of ancillary firms that provide vertical integrated services to few large firms in the region.

In Table 4.4, the determinants of the mean spatial effects of the first model shown in Fig. 4.1a are presented.[11] The R-square indicates that

---

[10] The role of financial constraints on the evolution of FSD is supported by Desai, Gompers and Lerner (2003). Similarly, Fazzari, Glenn Hubbard, and Petersen (1988) show that financial constraints influence a firm's investment decisions. Holtz-Eakin, Joulfaian, and Rosen (1994) test the role of liquidity constraints in the formation of new enterprises. Their analysis suggests that the size of inheritance has an effect on entrepreneurial choice and on the investment in the capital of a new enterprise. Evans and Jovanovic (1989) and Holtz-Eakin et al. (1994) show that the probability of survival depends on assets. Under an assumption that banks lend under the security of collateral, this suggests presence of credit-rationing. Hurst and Lusardi (2004) argue that households with higher levels of wealth have a higher tolerance for risk and are most likely to be business owners.

[11] The data on financial indicators for the regions, the per-capital net state domestic product (NSDP) come from the Reserve Bank of India's Handbook of Statistics on Indian Economy. The data on population density and size of the districts is taken from 2001 Census. The data on small

Table 4.4 Determinants of the mean spatial effects in Fig. 4.1 (*Start-up size given by initial fixed assets*)

Independent	I	II	III
Financial development			
Per-capita credit	0.155***		
	(0.032)		
Credit-deposit ratio		0.216***	
		(0.044)	
Per-Capita bank offices			0.173***
			(0.060)
Economic development			
Per-Capita NSDP	1.259***	1.274***	1.362***
	(0.079)	(0.077)	(0.075)
Unemployment	−0.0909***	−0.136***	−0.102***
	(0.029)	(0.029)	(0.029)
Literacy rate	0.00499*	0.00986***	0.00601**
	(0.0026)	(0.0025)	(0.0026)
Demographics			
Mid-size district	0.173***	0.160***	0.201***
	(0.055)	(0.055)	(0.056)
Large district	−0.0531	−0.0608	−0.0118
	(0.17)	(0.17)	(0.17)
Population density	−0.00409	0.0270	0.0328
	(0.028)	(0.027)	(0.028)
Agglomeration index			
Firm density	−0.412***	−0.393***	−0.398***
	(0.024)	(0.024)	(0.025)
Constant	−17.36***	−15.76***	−14.96***
	(0.73)	(0.76)	(1.00)
Observations	532	532	532
R^2	0.60	0.60	0.59
F	99.15	99.33	94.70
R^2 Adjusted	0.597	0.597	0.585

Notes: *Signifies $p < 0.05$; **Signifies $p < 0.01$; ***Signifies $p < 0.001$. Standard errors are reported in parentheses. Dependent variable is the mean spatial effect per district after estimation of the geoadditive models

close to 60% of the variation across space that remains after filtering the firm and industry effects can be explained by the regional variables discussed above. Financial development, measured by per-capita credit

firm density for constructing the agglomeration index is from the third census of small scale industries. The data on unemployment is based on the number of people registered at the employment exchanges.

flows, credit-deposit ratio in the region, and density of bank branches has a positive effect on the spatial patterns, suggesting that financial development increases the likelihood of a region having positive impact on the size of new firm start-ups. Economic development, measured by the per-capita net state domestic product, and literacy rate in the region have significant positive effects suggesting that spatial units that are more economically developed give birth to firm start-ups that have a larger size. The coefficient on the unemployment variable is negative and significant suggesting that unemployment in a region leads to new firm start-ups with a small size. The agglomeration index, given by the density of small firms in a region, is significantly negative indicating that concentration of a large number of small firms in a region gives birth to firms with smaller size.[12] The demographic variables are mostly insignificant. Thus, the estimation results suggest that the spatial patterns of firms' start-up size that remain after filtering the firm level and industry level effects, are attributable to a large extent to the variations in economic and financial development across spatial units. Table 4.5 explains the spatial effects of the second model, shown in Fig. 4.2a. The results confirm the effects of financial and economic development on start-up size.

4.3 Conclusion

A growing body of literature examines the determinants of firm size distribution and its evolution over time (Cabral & Mata, 2003; Angelini & Generale, 2008) and a component of this literature examines the determinants of the start-up size of firms (Mata & Machado, 1996; Colombo et al., 2004). This literature focuses mainly on the industry characteristics and personality traits of the entrepreneurs in explaining why initial size varies systematically across start-ups.

---

[12] This may reflect the presence of a large number of small ancillary firms providing services across the value chain to few large firms in the region.

Table 4.5 Determinants of the mean spatial effects in Fig. 4.2 (*Start-up size* given by initial employment)

Independent	I	II	III
Financial development			
Per-capita credit	0.0567***		
	(0.014)		
Credit-deposit ratio		0.112***	
		(0.019)	
Per-Capita bank offices			0.0385
			(0.027)
Economic development			
Per-Capita NSDP	0.243***	0.231***	0.285***
	(0.035)	(0.034)	(0.033)
Unemployment	−0.0517***	−0.0726***	−0.0564***
	(0.013)	(0.013)	(0.013)
Literacy rate	0.00331***	0.00530***	0.00404***
	(0.0011)	(0.0011)	(0.0012)
Demographics			
Mid-Size district	0.0396	0.0319	0.0470*
	(0.025)	(0.024)	(0.025)
Large district	0.0740	0.0704	0.0830
	(0.075)	(0.074)	(0.076)
Population density	−0.00749	0.00320	0.00582
	(0.013)	(0.012)	(0.012)
Agglomeration index			
Firm density	−0.179***	−0.173***	−0.171***
	(0.011)	(0.010)	(0.011)
Constant	−4.634***	−3.870***	−4.037***
	(0.32)	(0.33)	(0.45)
Observations	534	534	534
R^2	0.44	0.46	0.43
F	52.32	56.09	49.36
R^2 Adjusted	0.435	0.453	0.421

Notes: *Signifies $p < 0.05$; **Signifies $p < 0.01$; ***Signifies $p < 0.001$. Standard errors are reported in parentheses. Dependent variable is the posterior mean spatial effect district after estimation of the geoadditive models

In this chapter, a new database of entrants in India is analysed using geoadditive models to examine the link between geographic location and the size of new firm start-ups.

The empirical evidence presented here suggests that the spatial location is an important micro-determinant of the size of firm start-ups. In particular, spatial neighbourhood effects exert a strong influence on firm size at entry. The size of new firm start-ups exhibits remarkably distinct spatial patterns after filtering firm level and industry level effects. This also suggests that the right skewed nature of firm size distribution may be attributable to the emergence of many small firms in some regions.

For India, the results reveal a clear north-south divide in the size of new firm start-ups. The results provide important first insights identifying those factors shaping start-up size in the context of a developing economy. In particular, ownership structure and initial knowledge endowments are found to influence the size of new firms.

Furthermore, an investigation into the factors that shape these residual spatial patterns shows that variation in financial and economic development across regions, literacy rates, and the density of small firms in a district can explain, to a large extent, the spatial patterns of firms' start-up size that remain after filtering firm and industry level effects. Thus, regions that are more developed are found to give birth to superior start-ups.

References

Acs, Z. J., & Armington, C. (2006). *Entrepreneurship, geography, and American economic growth*. Cambridge University Press.

Angelini, P., & Generale, A. (2008). On the evolution of firm size distributions. *American Economic Review, 98*(1), 426–438.

Astebro, T., & Bernhardt, I. (2005). The winner's curse of human capital. *Small Business Economics, 24*, 63–78.

Audretsch, D. B. (1995). *Innovation and industry evolution*. Cambridge: MIT Press.

Audretsch, D. B., & Feldman, M. P. (1996). R&D spillovers and the geography of innovation and production. *American Economic Review, 86*(3), 630–640.

Audretsch, D. B., Keilbach, M., & Lehman, E. (2006). *Entrepreneurship and economic growth*. New York: Oxford University Press.

Audretsch, D. B., & Stephan, P. E. (1996). Company-scientist locational links: The case of biotechnology. *American Economic Review, 86*(4), 641–652.

Beck, T., Demirgüç-Kunt, A., & Levine, R. (2006). *Bank concentration, competition, and crises: First results. Journal of banking & finance, 30*(5), 1581–1603.

Burgess, R., & Pande, R. (2005). Do rural banks matter? Evidence from the Indian social banking experiment. *American Economic Review, 95*(3), 780–795.

Cabral, L. M. B., & Mata, J. (2003). On the evolution of the firm size distribution: Facts and theory. *The American Economic Review, 93*(4), 1075–1090.
Caves, R. E. (1998). Industrial organization and new findings on the turnover and mobility of firms. *Journal of Economic Literature, 36*(4), 1947–1982.
Colombo, M. G., Delmastro, M., & Grilli, L. (2004). Entrepreneurs' human capital and the start-up size of new technology-based firms. *International Journal of Industrial Organization, 22*, 1183–1211.
Colombo, M. G., & Grilli, L. (2005). Start-up size: The role of external financing. *Economic Letters, 88*, 243–250.
Desai, M., Gompers, P., & Lerner, J. (2003). *Institutions, capital constraints and entrepreneurial firm dynamics: Evidence from Europe*. Working Paper No. 10165, NBER, National Bureau of Economic Research. December.
Dunne, T., Roberts, M. J., & Samuelson, L. (1989). The growth and failure of U.S. manufacturing plants. *Quarterly Journal of Economics, 104*(4), 671–698.
Evans, D. S., & Jovanovic, B. (1989). An estimated model of entrepreneurial choice under liquidity constraints. *Journal of Political Economy, 97*(4), 808–827.
Fazzari, S. M., Glenn Hubbard, R., & Petersen, B. C. (1988). Financing constraints and corporate investment. *Brookings Papers on Economic Activity, 1988*(1), 141–206.
Geroski, P. A. (1995). What do we know about entry? *International Journal of Industrial Organization, 13*, 421–440.
Görg, H., & Ruane, F. (2000). Determinants of firm start-up size: An application of quantile regressions for Ireland. *Small Business Economics, 14*, 211–222.
Görg, H., & Strobl, E. (2002). Multinational companies and entrant start-up size: Evidence from quantile regressions. *Review of Industrial Organization, 20*, 15–31.
Griliches, Z. (1992). The search for R&D spillovers. *Scandinavian Journal of Economics, 94*, 29–47.
Holtz-Eakin, D., Joulfaian, D., & Rosen, H. S. (1994). Sticking it out: Entrepreneurial survival and liquidity constraints. *Journal of Political Economy, 102*(1), 53–75.
Hurst, E., & Lusardi, A. (2004). Liquidity constraints, household wealth, and entrepreneurship. *Journal of Political Economy, 112*(2), 319–347.
Jaffe, A. B. (1989). Real effects of academic research. *American Economic Review, 79*(5), 957–970.

Jaffe, A. B., Trajtenberg, M., & Henderson, R. (1993). Geographic localization of knowledge spillovers as evidenced in patent citations. *Quarterly Journal of Economics, 108*(3), 577–598.
Krugman, P. (1991a). History and industry location: The case of the manufacturing belt. *American Economic Review, 81*(2), 80–83.
Krugman, P. (1991b). Increasing returns and economic geography. *Journal of Political Economy, 99*(3), 483–499.
Levine, R. (1997). Financial development and economic growth: Views and agenda. *Journal of Economic Literature, 35*(2), 688–726.
Lucas, R. (1978). On the size distribution of business firms. *Bell Journal of Economics, 9*, 508–523.
Mata, J. (1996). Markct, cntrepreneurs and the size of new firms. *Economic Letters, 52*, 89–94.
Mata, J., & Machado, J. A. F. (1996). Firm start-up size: A conditional quantile approach. *European Economic Review, 40*, 1305–1323.
Mata, J., Portugal, P., & Guimaraes, P. (1995). The survival of new plants: Start-up conditions and post-entry evolution. *International Journal of Industrial Organization, 13*, 459–481.
Nurmi, S. (2006). Sectoral differences in plant start-up size in the Finnish economy. *Small Business Economics, 26*, 39–59.
Romer, P. M. (1986). Increasing returns and long-run growth. *Journal of Political Economy, 1986*(*94*), 1002–1037.
Romer, P. M. (1990). Endogenous technological change. *Journal of political Economy, 98*(5, Part 2), S71–S102.
Romer, P. M. (1994). The origins of endogenous growth. *Journal of Economic Perspectives, 8*(1), 3–22.

5

Firm Growth and Barriers to Growth Among Small Firms in India

5.1 Background

Given the special role of small businesses in providing economic opportunities for a large number of people, and the obstacles to growth that they encounter, developing countries have often taken a favourable position towards micro and small firms. India has, historically, been especially supportive of its small enterprises (Little, 1987). For example, the Indian government has granted exclusive production rights of certain goods and services to Small Scale Industry (SSI) businesses and, even though the Indian economy has undergone considerable deregulation in recent years, the production of many goods continues to be reserved for small businesses.[1]

It is estimated that, in 2001, the small-scale Industry in India[2] accounted for around 95% of the industrial units in the country, contributed 40% of the manufacturing sector output, and close to one-third of the India's exports (SIDBI, 2001). By 2009, the share of small-scale

[1] Most of these items are foodstuffs and consumer products. For a complete list of protected items, see http://www.smallindustryindia.com/publications/reserveditems/resvex.htm.

[2] Small Scale Industry comprises of small firms with an initial investment less than 10 million Indian rupees, an amount approximately equivalent to 200 thousand USD (http://www.dcmsme.gov.in/publications/circulars/circularmay1994.html#icoty, accessed on 25 October 2010).

J. P. Tamvada, *Microentrepreneurship in a Developing Country*,
https://doi.org/10.1007/978-3-030-68628-4_5

industry's contribution to manufacturing output increased to 45% and the share of exports rose to 40% (MSME, 2009).

Government support for micro and small firms, however, is not uncontroversial.[3] While some view entrepreneurship as the 'prime mover' which can initiate the development process (Leff, 1979), or as a means to attain a more efficient allocation of resources (You, 1995), others focus on the low productivity of these enterprises and are pessimistic about the role they can play in economic development.[4]

5.2 Factors Shaping Small Firm Growth

The emerging body of literature on opportunity and necessity entrepreneurship in developing countries suggests that although the magnitude of entrepreneurial activity is higher in developing countries, a significant proportion of entrepreneurs are driven by necessity (Acs, 2006; Wennekers, Van Stel, Thurik, & Reynolds, 2005). Recent work has found it useful to distinguish between firms on the basis of their growth performance. Roughly speaking, the intuition is that high productivity entrepreneurial firms will grow fast, while those who turn to self-employment simply because they have no other option are more interested in survival and remain at a small scale. For example, Rogerson (1996) distinguishes between 'survivalist' and other small firms, while Autio (2008) separates high aspiration entrepreneurs from low aspiration entrepreneurs. It

[3] For example, Beck, Demirguc-Kunt, and Levine (2005) examine the role of the small and medium enterprise sector in 45 countries (not including India). They begin by reviewing the prior literature and conclude, "firm-level studies do not provide an empirical foundation for subsidizing SMEs." (Beck et al. 2005, p. 201). In their empirical analysis, they observe a robust positive relationship between the relative size of the SME sector and economic growth, although the SME-growth relationship is not robust to the use of instrumental variables to control for endogeneity. Put differently, they write that "although a prosperous SME sector is a characteristic of flourishing economies, we cannot reject the view that SMEs do not cause growth." (p. 224). They also fail to observe any significant relationship between the size of the SME sector and poverty alleviation.

[4] As such, there is some skepticism about the economic foundations of government support of small enterprises—"India is ...exceptional in the extent and range of its policies that directly support SSEs. ...They have been romantic, rather than economic." (Little, 1987, p. 232). SSEs is an acronym for small scale enterprises.

should be noted that these classification schemes rest mainly on different growth performances of small firms.[5]

The negative dependence of growth on size is well documented in the literature, especially for small firms, and is taken by many authors as a 'stylized fact' (see Coad, 2009, Chapter 4, for a survey). We therefore hypothesize that smaller firms will grow faster in our database. A negative dependence of growth on age has been found by a long list of authors.[6] In the case of small firms in India, however, two recent studies (Das, 1995; Shanmugam & Bhaduri, 2002) observe that while larger firms have lower growth rates, age is significantly positively related to firm growth. Das (1995) examines the growth of firms in a young, fast-growing computer hardware industry in India, while Shanmugam and Bhaduri (2002) focus on a sample of 392 Indian manufacturing firms.

Although young firms have higher expected growth rates, they do not have an easy existence. They may well suffer from the "liability of newness" (Stinchcombe, 1965) and face difficulties because they lack experience and knowledge, and they have not yet been legitimated or recognized in the marketplace. In contrast to the liability of newness, however, it is useful to consider the concept of a 'liability of senescence' (Barron, West, & Hannan, 1994). This adversely affects old firms who, after years of repeating the same production routines and accumulated rules and structures, become more inert. Furthermore, there is the concept of 'liability of obsolescence' (Barron et al., 1994) which holds that older firms are no longer a good fit to the new market environment. Younger firms, on the other hand, are more flexible and can internalize outside knowledge in their routines. Although at first glance these perspectives appear to be conflicting, it is important to recognize the subtle differences between the

[5] This body of literature is also related to the debate on formal-informal labor markets in less developed countries and the nature of self-employment in such contexts (Blau, 1985; Fields, 2005; Günther & Launov, 2006; Harris & Todaro, 1970; Maloney, 2004; Tamvada, 2010).

[6] A negative relationship between age and growth has been found by Fizaine (1968) for French establishments, Dunne, Roberts, and Samuelson (1989) for US establishments, Evans (1987b); Evans (1987a) for US manufacturing firms, Variyam and Kraybill (1992) for US manufacturing and services firms, Liu, Tsou, and Hammitt (1999) for Taiwanese electronics plants, Sleuwaegen and Goedhuys (2002) for Ivorian manufacturing firms, Reichstein and Dahl (2004) for Danish limited liability companies, Geroski and Gugler (2004) for large European companies, and Yasuda (2005) for Japanese manufacturing firms.

liability of newness and the liabilities of senescence and obsolescence. Young firms are fragile and vulnerable, they are unable to weather adverse shocks, and they suffer from a lack of legitimation and recognition. For instance, in our 'barriers to growth' analysis, we would expect young firms to suffer from access to working capital (and we do in fact observe this). Old firms, in contrast, are more inert, and we would expect them to be less able to face new challenges (such as exporting) and to integrate new external knowledge into their production routines. We would therefore expect that old firms are less successful in converting export activity into growth, and in converting external knowhow into superior growth performance.

Further, there is ample evidence that female enterprises in developing countries experience slower growth than male enterprises (McPherson, 1996; Mead & Liedholm, 1998) presumably because of conservative social values and attitudes concerning women in industry (El-Namaki, 1988). Banerjee and Duflo (2007, p. 162) explain that "If you have few skills and little capital, and especially if you are a woman, being an entrepreneur is often easier than finding an employer with a job to offer." Female entrepreneurs in developing countries are less ambitious about growth and financial performance than their male counterparts are (Hisrich & Ozturk, 1999; Singh, Reynolds, & Muhammad, 2001). They are less concerned about achieving their high-growth business aspirations than they are about providing for their families. Female-led enterprises are typically smaller and pay less to their employees (Singh et al., 2001). We therefore anticipate that female firms will have lower growth rates, on average.

Many studies show that exporting has a positive impact on performance. As Grossman and Helpman (1991) suggest, foreign buyers may provide technical assistance to exporters leading to improved production efficiency. Clerides et al. (1998) show that international trade could improve firms' access to advanced technical knowledge. They find that firms that export are more productive than non-exporting firms in many developing countries. For these reasons, we expect a positive effect of exporting, and external knowledge on firm growth. However, we anticipate that these benefits of exporting and external knowhow will be stronger for younger firms than for older firms, who may well be too inert to benefit from these challenging opportunities.

Firms that enter small often remain small, because they face formidable barriers to growth. Indeed, several authors have commented on the "missing middle" in the firm size distribution that arises when large firms grow larger but small firms rarely grow into the next size category (Sleuwaegen & Goedhuys, 2002; Tybout, 2000). These enterprises remain small for a whole host of reasons such as continuing financial constraints, transport costs, limited infrastructure, and a lack of suitable management resources. In particular, difficulties in adopting new technologies and crossing over to the 'modern' sector have been singled out as impeding the growth of small firms in developing countries (Aftab & Rahim, 1989). In our analysis of questionnaire responses concerning perceived barriers to growth, we investigate which types of firm are more vulnerable to certain specific growth barriers. For example, we might expect that small and young firms are likely to have problems obtaining access to capital, while exporting firms might have problems in finding (skilled) employees.

5.3 Growth and Decline of Small Firms in India

In this section, we begin by describing the database used in this chapter, before presenting the distributions of some key variables and finally providing some summary statistics.

Previous work on entrepreneurship in developing countries has tended to use small samples obtained from correspondence with entrepreneurs through questionnaires. Undeniably, this approach has found valuable new results where data was sparse. In this chapter, however, we use a government census, and there is a very high response rate.[7] Our work thus complements previous work by providing estimates based on a large

[7] The survey was conducted on all registered small firms and was conducted by the office of the Development Commissioner, Government of India. According to the Development Commissioner, India, "All the SSI units permanently registered up to 31-3-2001 numbering 2,262,401 were surveyed on complete enumeration basis, of which 1,374,974 units (61%) were found to be working

database. We do not focus on the details and specificities of particular regions or categories of businesses, as other work has done, but instead provide an aggregate view of the characteristics of all Indian firms. Previous work focusing on small samples can thus be compared to our estimates. However, the estimates reported here have an advantage over much previous work because our large sample size ensures representativeness of our results.

The main source of data for examining the determinants of firm growth comes from the Ministry of Small Scale Industries in India. We use firm level data from the third census of registered small scale firms. This census was conducted for the financial year 2002–2003 (the reader interested in the macroeconomic context of our analysis is referred to other sources).[8] This rich dataset has data on 1.5 million small firms. In an attempt to have some degree of homogeneity between the firms we analyse, we restrict the sample to firms in the manufacturing sector. Each new firm was asked a series of questions such as its year of initial production, the sector of its operation, the source of its technical knowledge and energy, the gross output for three consecutive financial years, ownership type, and whether it experienced 'significant decline' over the last three years. If the firm experienced a decline, it was asked the causes for its decline. The sample contains new small firms (including those that are growing rapidly) as well as old firms that have not grown beyond the size threshold despite their age.[9]

---

and 887,427 units (39%) were found to be closed." (http://www.dcmsme.gov.in/ssiindia/census/highlights.htm, accessed on 25 October 2010).

[8] The rapid transformation of the Indian economy from a state-controlled license regime to a liberalized regime is widely documented in the literature (we refer the reader to Aghion, Burgess, Redding, & Zilibotti, 2005; Kochhar, Kumar, Rajan, Subramanian, & Tokatlidis, 2006; Rodrik & Subramanian, 2005). These economic transitions have had implications for industry wide productivity and competition (see Krishna & Mitra, 1998; Balakrishnan, Parameswaran, Pushpangadan, & Babu, 2006). India is the second most populated country in the world with a population exceeding one billion. For further indicators of economic development in India, such as GDP, life expectancy, literacy rates, inequality and the structure of Indian industry (shares of agriculture, industry and services) the reader is referred to Allen, Chakrabarti, De, Qian, and Qian (2006).

[9] The Ministry of Small Scale Industries defines firms having an initial investment less than 10 million Indian rupees as small and medium sized enterprises.

In theory, one might be concerned about the statistical effects of having an upper threshold on the sample. At the top of the distribution, near the threshold, relatively large firms may grow or decline. Growing firms might be excluded from the sample (because they exceed the threshold) whereas declining firms would stay in the sample. This might lead to a downward bias on the growth rates of large firms. In practice, however, this does not seem to be an important issue. First, only a very small proportion of firms are close to the upper size threshold. Second, firms are sorted according to their initial size (i.e. size at the beginning of production) rather than their final size, such that firms that are large enough to be near the threshold will not be censored even if their final size is above the threshold. Third, we repeated the analysis using a different (lower) size threshold and we obtained similar results.[10]

The main variables in the empirical analysis include age of firm, size (gross output), ownership type, gender of the entrepreneur, exporting status, source of technical knowhow and of course firm growth rates (calculated as log-differences of size). The control variables include industry dummies, sources of energy, and regional dummy variables. In keeping with previous studies, our measure of growth rates is calculated by taking the differences of the logarithms of size:

$$GROWTH_{it} = \log(X_{it}) - \log(X_{i,t-2}) \tag{5.1}$$

where X represents firm size and is measured in terms of gross output.[11]

We now present some univariate distributions of some of the main variables.

Figure 5.1 shows the size and age distributions for the small businesses in our sample. The size distribution (Fig. 5.1; left) shows a smooth

[10] By upper threshold we refer to the upper limit of the investment of 10 million Indian rupees that is used to define small scale firms in India. In order to check for the robustness of the results, we artificially lower this threshold to exclude firms that have initial investment greater than 9 million Indian rupees, and find that the results are consistent.

[11] Growth is measured in terms of changes in gross output, rather than in terms of an alternative measure of firm size such as number of employees, because of data constraints. For example, we only have data on firm employment levels for the single financial year 2001–02, which means it is not possible to calculate employment growth rates.

unimodal shape, which is in line with the previous literature on firm size distributions. There is a concave decay on the upper tail, which indicates that the firm size distribution has a faster decay than the Pareto benchmark.[12] Although there is an upper size threshold which determines whether or not firms are required to answer the questionnaire, this threshold does not produce any dramatic cut-off point at the upper end of the size distribution.[13]

The age distribution is shown in (Fig. 5.1; right). Empirical age distributions are hard to find in the literature, presumably because data on age is not always easy to obtain (but for an early contribution see Huergo and Jaumandreu (2004); see also Coad (2010) for a survey). Our plot of the firm age distribution is therefore a useful addition to this nascent strand of literature. Most of the businesses are young, the median age being 12 years and 75% of the businesses being 18 or younger. The decay in the distribution is roughly linear over most of the support, which allows us to speculate that an exponential law would be a suitable representation.[14]

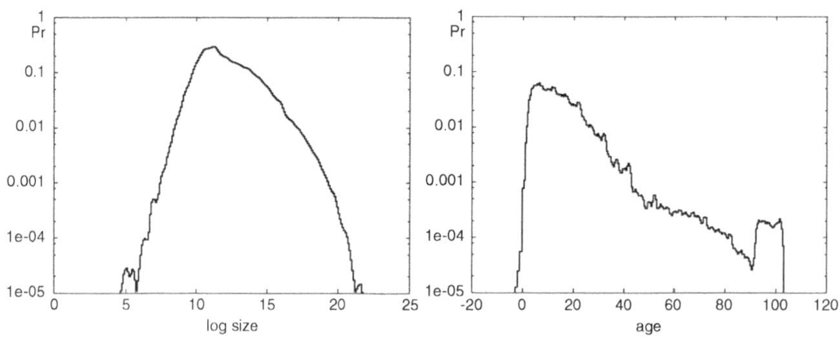

Fig. 5.1 Kernel densities of the size distribution (log output in the financial year 1999–2000; left) and age distribution (right), both plotted with a logarithmic *y*-axis. Kernel densities are computed for equispaced points using an Epanenchnikov kernel (using the gbutils 5.1 software package)

[12] The Pareto distribution (also known as a power law distribution) can be represented as a straight line of negative slope on log-log axes.

[13] By definition all firms in the survey have an investment in fixed assets in plant and machinery that is less than Rs 10 million. This is the upper threshold for firms' getting classified under Small Scale Industry in India at the time when the survey was conducted.

[14] Incidentally, this lends some support to the assumption of an exponential distribution of firm age in the model of the firm size distribution in Coad (2009). In this model, the lognormal distribution

There is a local peak at around 100 years, however, which is relatively insignificant in magnitude although it is clearly discernable when logarithmic axes are used. This local peak could be due to misreporting, as firms approximate their age to a century.[15]

Looking at the growth rate distribution, we are in fact able to detect an unnaturally high occurrence of tenfold growth rates when the data are plotted on logarithmic axes (see Fig. 5.2, right) although these local peaks are barely visible on standard axes (see Fig. 5.2, left). We conclude that measurement error and data entry mistakes are present in our dataset (this is discussed in more depth in the methodology section).

Summary statistics for our database are presented in Table 5.1.[16] The summary statistics in Table 5.1 show that the average age of a firm in the sample is 13.9 years. The average annual growth rate is between 6–7%. Single ownership is the most prevalent form of firm ownership structure. 86.5% of the firms are owned by proprietary owners and 9.2% of the firms are partnerships. Only 8% of the firms are managed by women entrepreneurs. While 70% of the firms in the sample have electricity as the main source of power, 19.7% firms do not use any source of power, 6% of firms depend on coal and oil and 3.3% of firms use non-conventional and traditional sources of power such as firewood.

It is likely that there are several sources of measurement error. Although this survey is considered to be an authoritative source of information that has been used to guide industrial policy in India, it cannot be expected that the records are 100% accurate. First, there may well be data entry problems. For example, if the data is mistakenly entered with an extra 'zero', or if a digit is accidentally omitted, then the firm will experience a tenfold growth rate (positive or negative growth). Second, although all

---

of firm size obtained from a Gibrat process is mixed with an exponential firm age distribution to obtain the Pareto firm size distribution suggested by a number of empirical studies.

[15] Self-reported data on the age of small businesses has been described by Phillips and Kirchhoff (1989) as being less than perfectly reliable, even in developed countries such as the US. In the case of India, it should be remembered that many *people* don't know exactly how old they are! As such, there may well be a small degree of measurement error in the age distribution, and as a result we don't seek to explain every feature of this distribution, but at this preliminary stage we merely emphasize the broad shape of the distribution. For instance, the age distribution as represented in Fig. 5.1 is powerful enough to quickly dispel the myth that all small firms are young.

[16] In our baseline sample (e.g. in Table 5.2 column (2)) we have around 700'000 observations.

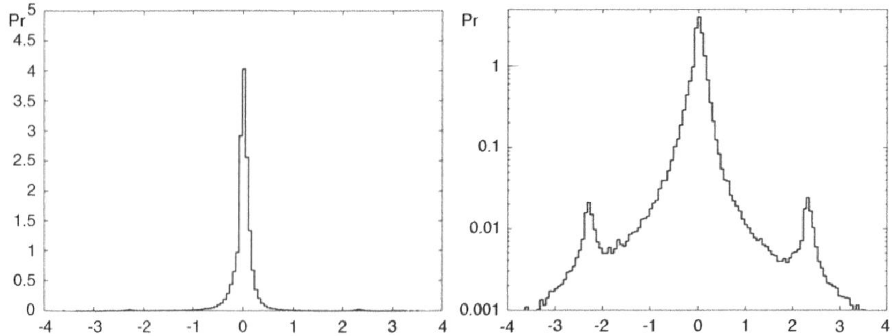

Fig. 5.2 Annual growth rate distributions (i.e. (log) growth of output from financial year 2000–01 to FY 2001–02) for the raw dataset (i.e. before trimming), plotted on a linear *y*-axis (left) or a logarithmic *y*-axis (right). Note the local peaks in the right-hand figure at $\pm\log_e 10 = \pm 2.303$, which correspond to tenfold growth rates. Kernel densities are computed for equispaced points using an Epanenchnikov kernel (using the gbutils 5.1 software package)

the firms in the database are registered small firms, some of them do not keep detailed accounts of their activities, and so their responses may not be entirely accurate.

The growth rate distribution presented earlier in Fig. 5.2 suggests that our data contains a non-negligible amount of measurement error in the form of data entry mistakes. The growth rate distribution, when plotted with a logarithmic y-axis, displays local peaks at $\pm\log_e 10 = \pm 2.303$, which correspond to tenfold growth rates. This unusually high frequency of tenfold growth events is at odds with the existing literature on firm growth rate distributions,[17] and we suggest that it is due to misreporting and data entry mistakes (e.g. tenfold growth would occur if the figure for gross output in any year contains an extra digit (e.g. 500000 instead of 50000), or a digit is missing (e.g. 5000 instead of 50000). Therefore, we have shown that by examining the growth rate distribution one can make deductions about the likely presence of outliers.

To take these caveats into account, we trim our dataset for outliers. In our main specification, we omit firms experiencing growth rates that are

[17] Previous work on growth rate distributions has suggested that the empirical distribution is well approximated by a unimodal 'tent-shape' distribution, in particular, the Laplace (or symmetric exponential) distribution. For a survey of growth rate distributions, see Coad (2009, Chapter 3).

Table 5.1 Descriptive statistics-all firms

	Mean	Std. Dev.	Min	Max
Growth 2002/01–2000/99	0.1441	0.2305	−0.9609	0.9651
Ln (Output 2002/01)	12.1283	1.7553	0.6931	22.7830
Ln (Output 2001/00)	12.0614	1.7571	0.6931	22.8357
Ln (Output 2000/99)	11.9842	1.7610	0.6931	22.7388
Age	13.9261	10.2137	1	102
Ln (Age)	2.4031	0.6989	0	4.6250
Proprietary ownership	0.8646	0.3422	0	1
Partnership	0.0918	0.2887	0	1
Private company	0.0299	0.1702	0	1
Co-operative	0.0036	0.0601	0	1
Other ownership	0.0102	0.1004	0	1
Woman	0.0809	0.2728	0	1
Knowhow from abroad	0.0103	0.1011	0	1
Knowhow from domestic sources	0.1418	0.3488	0	1
No power	0.1966	0.3975	0	1
Coal	0.0242	0.1536	0	1
Oil	0.0362	0.1867	0	1
LPG	0.0060	0.0775	0	1
Electricity	0.7041	0.4565	0	1
Non-conventional energy	0.0045	0.0670	0	1
Firewood	0.0284	0.1661	0	1
Rural	0.4189	0.4934	0	1
Export	0.0070	0.0836	0	1
N	671159			

greater than 400% in magnitude.[18] Furthermore, we use median regression (also known as Least Absolute Deviation regression, or the L_1 estimator) which performs better than OLS in the case of non-Gaussian distributions of the dependent variable. While least-squares estimators minimize the sum of squared residuals, median regressions minimize the sum of absolute residuals. Median regressions have indeed been popular in growth rate regressions because of the heavy-tailed and non-Gaussian nature of growth rate distributions (see e.g. Bottazzi, Coad, Jacoby, and Secchi 2010; Coad 2007). However, in a robustness analysis we also investigate OLS estimates (not reported). Generally, these tend to be similar to median regression results. To reduce the influence of unreliable

[18] In further analysis (not reported here) we also explored the robustness of our results using a 200% growth cut-off point, and obtained similar results.

data, we also smooth our growth rate variable by measuring growth over a two-year period (from financial year 1999–2000 to financial year 2001–2002), not just one year, so that the impact of short-term growth shocks can be smoothed out.[19]

Extreme observations on the dependent variable (i.e. 'outliers') are therefore dealt with by removing extreme growth events, and by using an estimator that is robust to outliers. A further complication, however, is that there may well be extreme observations in the predictor space (i.e. 'leverage points'). Indeed, we have no reason to suspect that mismeasurement and data entry mistakes are exclusive concerns of the dependent variable and not the explanatory variables. We are also aware that standard regression techniques such as least-squares estimators and also median regressions (i.e. LAD-Least Absolute Deviation regressions) are highly sensitive to extreme observations in the form of leverage points (Rousseeuw & Leroy, 1987). In contrast, Least Median of Squares (LMS) regression is very robust to outliers and leverage points (Western, 1995), although some drawbacks are that LMS is computationally intensive (Rousseeuw & Leroy, 1987), and that standard errors cannot be computed for the coefficient estimates (Blasnik, 1998; Thorson, 1994). In order to detect extreme observations on the explanatory variables, we perform Least Median of Squares (LMS) regressions, and then inspect the LMS residuals. We then remove those observations that have LMS residuals with magnitudes greater than 2.5 standard deviations (i.e. the cut-off point suggested in Rousseeuw & Leroy, 1987, p17). This removes about 3.5% of our observations.[20] Once these outliers have been removed, we perform LAD regressions on the remaining observations. Our methodology therefore bears similarities to the Reweighted Least Squares estimator which gives weights of zero to leverage points (cf Rousseeuw & Leroy, 1987) and also to the Weighted LAD estimator in Giloni, Simonoff, and Sengupta (2006).

We now estimate the following firm growth equation for our cross-sectional dataset:

---

[19] A similar approach can be found in e.g. Liu et al., 1999.

[20] For example, without removing outliers we would have 695757 observations in Column 2 of Table 5.3, but when outliers are removed we have 671159 observations. This corresponds to a loss of 3.535% of observations.

$$\begin{aligned} Firm\,Growth = {} & \alpha + \beta 1 \times Size + \beta 2 \times Age + \beta 3 \times \mathrm{Pr}oprietary\,Ownership \\ & + \beta 4 \times Woman + \beta 5 \times Power\ Source + \beta 6 \times Technical\ Knowledge \\ & + \beta 7 \times Industrial \times Sector + \beta 8 \times Rural + \beta 9 \times Export \\ & + \beta 10 \times Regional\ Dummies + \varepsilon \end{aligned}$$

The main explanatory variables of interest are firm size, firm age, a dummy variable for female-owned firms, the power source of the firm, the use of external technical knowledge, and dummies for rural firms and for exporting firms. We include a full set of industry and regional dummies as control variables, although the coefficients are not reported in the results tables. More information on these variables can be found in the variables definition table in the Appendix (see Table 5.5).

We present the estimation results for the whole sample in Table 5.2, and the estimation results for the subsample of female firms in Table 5.3. In both tables, the basic specification estimating the effect of age and size on growth is presented in column (1). In column (2), we introduce the ownership variable 'proprietary', female, the knowledge source variables 'abroad' and 'domestic', export and rural location variables, and a set of industry and regional dummies. In column (3), we restrict the sample to young firms, that is, firms that are less than or equal to ten years old. In column (4), we restrict the sample to firms that are older than 10 years. In column (5), we restrict the sample to firms that are older than 20 years.

In order to make the results more digestible, we organize the results by first discussing age effects, then the results concerning female entrepreneurs, then the results concerning exporting and internalization of foreign knowledge, and finally proprietary ownership. Thus, the discussion of our empirical results is organized according to four main themes: firm age, female entrepreneurs, exporting and overseas knowledge, and proprietary ownership.

5.3.1 Size and Age

As seen in all specifications in Table 5.2, size and age have a negative association with firm growth. In other words, smaller, younger firms are expected to grow faster. Our estimates suggest that a

Table 5.2 Determinants of firm growth

	(1)	(2)	(3)	(4)	(5)
	All firms	All firms	Young firms	Old firms	Oldest firms
Variables			Age <= 10	Age > 10	Age > 20
Log(output)	−0.0114***	−0.0159***	−0.0164***	−0.0158***	−0.0146***
	(0.000129)	(0.000170)	(0.000275)	(0.000224)	(0.000341)
Log(age)	−0.00876***	−0.0133***	−0.0207***	−0.00733***	−0.00675***
	(0.000324)	(0.000343)	(0.000837)	(0.000822)	(0.00161)
Ownership					
Proprietary		−0.00358***	−0.00509***	−0.00220**	−0.00111
		(0.000743)	(0.00119)	(0.000977)	(0.00145)
Female		−0.00381***	−0.00403***	−0.00329***	−0.00609***
		(0.000877)	(0.00127)	(0.00127)	(0.00217)
Knowledge source					
Abroad		−0.00513**	0.00265	−0.0106***	−0.00136
		(0.00228)	(0.00368)	(0.00297)	(0.00489)
Domestic		−0.00227***	−0.000462	−0.00367***	−0.00717***
		(0.000676)	(0.00108)	(0.000894)	(0.00140)
Firm Characteristics					
Rural		−0.00367***	−0.00731***	−0.000985	0.000368
		(0.000522)	(0.000821)	(0.000700)	(0.00115)
Export		0.0537***	0.0672***	0.0462***	0.0451***
		(0.00278)	(0.00460)	(0.00358)	(0.00515)
Power Source					
Coal		−0.00863***	−0.0112***	−0.00856***	−0.00850***
		(0.00164)	(0.00319)	(0.00196)	(0.00270)
Oil		0.00570***	0.00337	0.00837***	0.00264
		(0.00145)	(0.00225)	(0.00195)	(0.00355)
LPG		0.0206***	0.0166***	0.0242***	0.0202***
		(0.00302)	(0.00453)	(0.00421)	(0.00661)
Electricity		0.0166***	0.0187***	0.0146***	0.0152***
		(0.000721)	(0.00112)	(0.000970)	(0.00158)
Non-conventional		0.0269***	0.0359***	0.0212***	0.0211***
		(0.00345)	(0.00534)	(0.00467)	(0.00808)
Firewood		0.00266*	0.00874***	−0.000256	0.000206
		(0.00152)	(0.00246)	(0.00198)	(0.00305)
Industry dummies		Yes	Yes	yes	Yes
Region dummies		Yes	Yes	Yes	Yes
Constant	0.301***	0.354***	0.380***	0.333***	0.314***
	(0.00172)	(0.00277)	(0.00459)	(0.00413)	(0.00761)

(continued)

Table 5.2 (continued)

	(1)	(2)	(3)	(4)	(5)
	All firms	All firms	Young firms	Old firms	Oldest firms
Variables			Age <= 10	Age > 10	Age > 20
Observations	671,159	671,159	291,466	379,693	128,150
Pseudo *R* Squared	0.0065	0.0343	0.0366	0.0328	0.0358

Notes: Standard errors in parentheses, $***p < 0.01$, $**p < 0.05$, $*p < 0.1$. Dependent variable is growth rate over three annual exercises (from 1999–2000 till 2001–2002). Firms experiencing more than fourfold growth are excluded. The base category for ownership type is 'other' which includes partnership firms and co-operatives, for knowledge source it is 'none', for power source it is 'no power'

one-standard-deviation increase in size results in a decrease of 2.76 percentage points in the growth rate.[21]

The finding of a negative dependence of growth on age is thus able to reconcile the dynamics of Indian small firms to the broad regularities observed in the rest of the world (as mentioned in Sect. 5.2). Further, as the statistically significant and negative coefficients of variable 'rural' in columns 3, 4, 5 of Table 5.2 suggest, young rural firms experience slower growth than older rural firms, perhaps because they have trouble establishing themselves in a rural setting.

Age, it seems, has a retarding effect on growth, but this retarding effect fades for firms above a certain age threshold. Put differently, young firms grow faster than older firms, but among a sample of old firms, growth becomes less dependent on age. As such, our results are similar to those obtained by Bigsten and Gebreeyesus (2007), who analyze Ethiopian census data on manufacturing firms with over 10 employees. Bigsten and Gebreeyesus (2007) observe. "[g]rowth and age are inversely related only in the first few years after entry and stay constant for most of the age group until it starts to have a positive relation beyond age 50." (p. 831).

[21] This estimate is calculated as follows. From the summary statistics table (Table 5.1) we observe that the standard deviation of log(output) is 1.7610. Now, from column (2) of Table 5.2 we see that the coefficient on log(output) is −0.0159. Ceteris paribus, changing log(output) by one standard deviation changes the dependent variable by 1.761 * −0.0159 = −0.0279999. The dependent variable is $\log_e$(growth rate), and the change in $\log_e$(growth rate) is = −0.0279999. A log(growth rate) of −0.0279999 corresponds to a (conventionally measured) growth rate of −0.0276115 (given that e^(−0.0279999) −1 = −0.0276115), which can then be rounded to −2.76%.

Table 5.3 Determinants of firm growth (subsample of female firms)

	(1)	(2)	(3)	(4)	(5)
	All firms	All firms	Young firms	Old firms	Oldest firms
Variables			Age <= 10	Age > 10	Age > 20
Log(output)	−0.0140***	−0.0188***	−0.0182***	−0.0192***	−0.0198***
	(0.000508)	(0.000732)	(0.00110)	(0.00100)	(0.00203)
Log(age)	−0.00330**	−0.0146***	−0.0183***	−0.0106***	−0.00714
	(0.00129)	(0.00149)	(0.00323)	(0.00384)	(0.00993)
Proprietary		−0.0174***	−0.0169***	−0.0153***	−0.00907
		(0.00330)	(0.00495)	(0.00447)	(0.00866)
Knowledge Source					
Abroad		−0.0156*	0.0120	−0.0283**	−0.0586**
		(0.00929)	(0.0150)	(0.0117)	(0.0266)
Domestic		0.00480*	0.00673	0.000592	−0.00280
		(0.00281)	(0.00417)	(0.00385)	(0.00814)
Firm Characteristics					
Rural		0.000593	−0.00207	0.00233	0.00354
		(0.00224)	(0.00321)	(0.00322)	(0.00744)
Export		0.0596***	0.105***	0.0475***	0.0740***
		(0.0110)	(0.0188)	(0.0134)	(0.0261)
Power Source					
Coal		−0.0321***	−0.0150	−0.0343***	−0.00293
		(0.00957)	(0.0167)	(0.0115)	(0.0223)
Oil		−0.0165**	−0.0207*	−0.00912	−0.00591
		(0.00755)	(0.0113)	(0.0103)	(0.0242)
LPG		0.0240**	0.0352**	0.00755	0.00919
		(0.0109)	(0.0146)	(0.0175)	(0.0368)
Electricity		0.0111***	0.0105***	0.0116***	0.0327***
		(0.00277)	(0.00386)	(0.00417)	(0.00978)
Non-conventional		0.0120	0.0370**	−0.0410**	−0.0108
		(0.0122)	(0.0169)	(0.0183)	(0.0394)
Firewood		0.00768	0.00799	0.00662	−0.00719
		(0.00548)	(0.00797)	(0.00780)	(0.0169)
Industry dummies		Yes	Yes	Yes	Yes
Region dummies		Yes	Yes	Yes	Yes
Constant	0.298***	0.391***	0.396***	0.379***	0.341***
	(0.00632)	(0.0118)	(0.0185)	(0.0186)	(0.0457)
Observations	54,330	54,330	30,488	23,842	6,658
Pseudo *R*-Squared	0.0072	0.0469	0.0507	0.0449	0.0447

Notes: Standard errors in parentheses, ***$p < 0.01$, **$p < 0.05$, *$p < 0.1$. Dependent variable is growth rate over three annual exercises (from 1999–2000 till 2001–2002). Firms experiencing more than fourfold growth are excluded. The base category for ownership type is 'other' which includes partnership firms and co-operatives, for knowledge source it is 'none', for power source it is 'no power'

In our baseline regression specification (Table 5.2), younger firms experience higher growth rates, even in the subsample of firms above 20 years old. For the subsample of female firms, however (Table 5.3) the negative dependence of growth on age is not significant, perhaps because these firms face formidable barriers to growth irrespective of their age.

As the significant coefficient on the variable 'firewood' in column (3) suggests, among young firms under 10, being a firewood firm has a positive impact on firm growth, while among 'old' firms over 20, as the coefficient in columns 4, 5 show, growth rates of firewood firms are expected to be lower. It could be that for firewood firms in particular, the advantages of experience are not great (because of a basic production technology) and youthful 'spunk' counts a lot more in determining success in this industry.

The results presented in Table 5.2 are consistent with the theory of 'liability of senescence' (Barron et al., 1994) because we observe statistically significant negative coefficients on the knowledge source variables 'Abroad' in column 4 suggesting that old firms are less capable of learning from foreign knowledge sources and translating them into superior growth. The coefficients for the 'export' variable in columns 3 is larger than the coefficient in column 5 suggesting that younger exporting firms enjoy greater growth rates than older exporting firms. The coefficient of exporting decreases dramatically (by over 30% in Table 5.2) as we move from young firms (less than ten years in column 3) to older firms (greater than 20 years in column 5).

5.3.2 Female Entrepreneurs

The results in Table 5.2 consistently show that firms headed by females grow slower, a finding that is consistent with a number of other studies. The coefficient of the variable 'female' is −0.00381 in column 2 of Table 5.2, which corresponds to a decrease in the expected growth rate of 0.380 percentage points (i.e. not exactly 0.381 percentage points, because our dependent variable is expressed in terms of logarithms).

One possible explanation could be that women self-select themselves into low growth industries. The existing literature, however, does not favour this interpretation. Mead and Liedholm (1998) survey the literature on female entrepreneurs in developing countries and conclude that female-led businesses have both lower survival probabilities and lower expected growth rates, even after controlling for other relevant factors. Furthermore, we observe a negative effect of female ownership on firm growth even after controlling for other factors such as industry and regional characteristics in Table 5.2.

However, the effect of interaction of 'female' variable with other variables on firm growth is not clear (see Table 5.2). For example, Table 5.2 does not allow us to examine the impact of a female business that is in a rural area, or a female business that exports. For this reason, in Table 5.3 we estimate all the specifications for a subsample of firms that are owned and managed by women entrepreneurs.

As the negative and statistically significant coefficients of 'abroad' in columns 4, 5 of Table 5.3 show, old female businesses that have a foreign knowledge source actually find it harder to grow, while this has no significant effect for younger female firms. As the positive and significant coefficients on 'export' variable in all the columns of Table 5.3 suggest, female firms of all ages stand to gain a lot from exporting. The effect of exporting on growth is stronger for female firms than for other firms when we compare the coefficients in Tables 5.2 and 5.3. Thus, once women are able to overcome the considerable difficulties associated with entering export markets, female-led firms are in a position to enjoy faster growth.

5.3.3 Exporting and Overseas Knowledge

In the case of female firms, it is the younger firms (with age 10 or less) that are better able to use both domestic knowledge sources to their advantage (the coefficient of 'domestic' in column 3, Table 5.3, is positive and significant at the 10% level). In contrast, there are a few cases whereby external sources of knowledge are observed to have a negative association with firm growth in the case of old firms, as in the case of old female firms using knowledge from abroad (Table 5.3, columns 4, 5) and in old firms using domestic knowledge (Table 5.2, columns 4, 5).

Exporting is observed to have a positive effect on growth in all specifications. Due to data limitations, we are unable to investigate whether it is fast-growth firms that self-select into export markets, or whether firms experience faster growth once they begin to export. Evidence on the productivity growth of firms in 4 African countries, however, suggests that learning-by-exporting effects are predominant, and that self-selection of the more productive firms into exporting plays no major role (Bigsten et al., 2004). The estimation results in Tables 5.2 and 5.3 suggest that the coefficient on exporting is larger for younger firms (in column 3) than the coefficient for older firms (in columns 4, 5), indicating that younger firms benefit more from exporting than their older counterparts. This is consistent with learning theories of firm growth via internationalization, which consider that entrepreneurial dynamism and vision are more important factors affecting export success than age and experience. In this view, older firms suffer from cognitive inertia that makes them less responsive to business opportunities and changing market conditions (Autio, Sapienza, & Almeida, 2000).

5.3.4 Proprietary Ownership

Our database also distinguishes between firms established as partnerships or under proprietary ownership. In our baseline results table (Table 5.2) as well as in the results for female firms (Table 5.3), we observe that proprietary firms have lower expected growth rates.

More specifically, we observe that, among young firms, proprietary firms face lower expected growth rates, although proprietary ownership has no significant association with growth among older firms (this can be seen by comparing the coefficients of the proprietary ownership variable in columns 3 and 5, in Tables 5.2 and 5.3).

5.4 Barriers to Growth

In this section, we focus on a subsample of declining firms. The questionnaire contains questions that relate specifically to declining firms and the specific obstacles to growth faced by these firms. In a first stage, firms are identified as declining firms if their net worth in the financial year 2001–2002 is less than 50% of their net worth in 2000–2001, if there has been a continuous delay in the payment of interest on the loans during the last year, or if there has been continuous decline in the output in the period 2000–2002. In the database, roughly 1 in 7 firms is classified as a 'declining firm'. In a second stage, these declining firms are given a list of eight reasons for their poor performance, and asked to identify which are the most important factors. These eight factors are the following: lack of demand, shortage of working capital, unavailability of raw materials, power shortage, labour problems, marketing problems, equipment problems, and management problems.

In Table 5.4, we estimate the internal determinants of (subjectively perceived) growth problems that these firms face. For the estimation results reported in Table 5.4, our dependent variable takes the value of 1 if firms report suffering from a particular growth barrier, and 0 otherwise. Our approach is similar to that of Sleuwaegen and Goedhuys (2002) for Ivorian firms and that of Robson and Obeng (2008) who analyze Ghanaian firms. The main problems for large firms seem to be labor problems and market problems. In contrast, small firms are more vulnerable to a lack of demand, problems obtaining working capital, problems of power shortages, equipment problems, and management problems. Old firms also suffer from labour and market problems, and in addition, they are susceptible to a lack of demand and problems with raw materials. Young firms, in contrast, have problems obtaining working capital. Proprietary firms have many of the opposite problems to old firms, in the sense that they have no problems concerning lack of demand or raw materials, but they do have difficulties obtaining working capital. The main problems faced by female firms seem to concern raw materials, and market problems. Rural firms are vulnerable to problems concerning raw materials, equipment, management, and also power shortages, while they are relatively less exposed to problems concerning labour and lack of

Table 5.4 Barriers to growth—probit regressions

	(1)	(2)	(3)	(4)	(5)	(6)	(7)	(8)
Barrier	Lack of	Working	Raw	Power	Labour	Market	Equipment	Management
	Demand	Capital	Materials	Shortage	Problems	Problems	Problems	Problems
Log(output)	−0.0477***	−0.0194***	0.00951**	−0.0139***	0.0438***	0.0331***	−0.0506***	−0.0246***
	(0.00316)	(0.00313)	(0.00396)	(0.00373)	(0.00479)	(0.00315)	(0.00474)	(0.00578)
Log(age)	0.0718***	−0.0842***	0.0543***	−0.00922	0.0383***	0.0206***	0.0454***	0.0138
	(0.00685)	(0.00678)	(0.00863)	(0.00825)	(0.0105)	(0.00680)	(0.00986)	(0.0123)
Ownership								
Proprietary	−0.0476***	0.0538***	−0.0654***	0.0332**	0.0553***	−0.0233*	−0.0619***	−0.103***
	(0.0140)	(0.0139)	(0.0177)	(0.0162)	(0.0207)	(0.0140)	(0.0206)	(0.0246)
Female	0.00327	0.0222	0.0860***	−0.0305	0.0144	0.0397***	0.0207	0.0258
	(0.0150)	(0.0147)	(0.0183)	(0.0193)	(0.0234)	(0.0147)	(0.0212)	(0.0264)
Knowledge Source								
Abroad	−0.173***	0.120**	0.104*	0.0113	0.0513	−0.0859*	0.0917	−0.105
	(0.0466)	(0.0470)	(0.0573)	(0.0526)	(0.0671)	(0.0474)	(0.0653)	(0.0909)
Domestic	−0.0520***	0.0819***	0.0375**	0.136***	0.114***	0.112***	0.152***	0.0192
	(0.0123)	(0.0122)	(0.0154)	(0.0141)	(0.0178)	(0.0122)	(0.0168)	(0.0219)
Firm Characteristics								
Rural	−0.0356***	0.00393	0.102***	0.180***	−0.0563***	−0.0550***	0.0967***	0.0394**
	(0.0103)	(0.0102)	(0.0128)	(0.0126)	(0.0161)	(0.0102)	(0.0146)	(0.0186)
Export	−0.0472	−0.0777*	0.00758	−0.180***	0.227***	−0.0825*	0.194***	0.105
	(0.0459)	(0.0457)	(0.0583)	(0.0554)	(0.0568)	(0.0464)	(0.0640)	(0.0755)
Power Source								
Coal	−0.0810**	0.0782**	0.240***	0.325***	0.00288	0.0726**	−0.112**	−0.109*
	(0.0336)	(0.0343)	(0.0389)	(0.0550)	(0.0554)	(0.0334)	(0.0521)	(0.0627)

(continued)

Table 5.4 (continued)

	(1)	(2)	(3)	(4)	(5)	(6)	(7)	(8)
Barrier	Lack of	Working	Raw	Power	Labour	Market	Equipment	Management
	Demand	Capital	Materials	Shortage	Problems	Problems	Problems	Problems
Oil	−0.184***	−0.00836	0.0738*	0.775***	0.0868	0.0158	0.0267	0.0664
	(0.0351)	(0.0362)	(0.0402)	(0.0442)	(0.0528)	(0.0351)	(0.0471)	(0.0585)
LPG	−0.106*	−0.0521	−0.102	0.666***	−0.171	0.132**	0.201***	−0.0684
	(0.0556)	(0.0552)	(0.0704)	(0.0784)	(0.107)	(0.0544)	(0.0752)	(0.104)
Electricity	−0.111***	−0.0668***	−0.0949***	1.270***	0.0977***	−0.0946***	0.0550***	−0.0501**
	(0.0139)	(0.0137)	(0.0167)	(0.0240)	(0.0224)	(0.0136)	(0.0196)	(0.0246)
Non-conventional	−0.456***	0.179**	0.0756	0.512***	−0.0637	−0.0864	−0.0521	−0.00519
	(0.0735)	(0.0758)	(0.0825)	(0.103)	(0.117)	(0.0716)	(0.0992)	(0.125)
Firewood	−0.158***	−0.0114	0.0590*	0.332***	0.169***	0.160***	−0.0379	0.00881
	(0.0266)	(0.0260)	(0.0308)	(0.0459)	(0.0412)	(0.0259)	(0.0397)	(0.0466)
Industry &	Yes	Yes	Yes	Yes	Yes	Yes	Yes	Yes
Region dummies	Yes	Yes	Yes	Yes	Yes	Yes	Yes	Yes
Constant	0.518***	0.654***	−1.308***	−1.670***	−2.517***	−0.888***	−0.776***	−1.557***
	(0.0526)	(0.0522)	(0.0657)	(0.0641)	(0.0819)	(0.0526)	(0.0759)	(0.0961)
Observations	84,595	84,602	84,544	84,491	84,446	84,590	84,413	84,441
Pseudo *R*-Squared	0.0721	0.0382	0.0472	0.1450	0.0457	0.0375	0.0324	0.0265

Dependent variable is a binary variable, taking the value 1 if the suggested factor is identified as a growth barrier and 0 otherwise. The sample is restricted to declining firms. Firms are considered to be declining if their net worth in 2001–2002 is less than 50% of their net worth in 2000–2001 or if there has been a continuous delay in the payment of interest on the loans during the last year or if there has been continuous decline in the output in the period 2000–2002. The base category for ownership type is 'other' which includes partnership firms and co-operatives, for knowledge source it is 'none', for power source it is 'no power' demand (i.e. relative to their urban counterparts). Exporting firms, on the other hand, cite labour problems as being particularly severe (perhaps because they need specialized skilled labour) as well as equipment problems, while power shortages are relatively unproblematic.

5.5 Conclusion

The aim of this chapter was to complement the literature that exists on the nature and performance of small businesses in developing countries. Using a unique large-scale database on small firms in India, the results are fairly representative of the structure of small business in India, and the results may also presumably be useful in understanding what happens in other developing countries.

The presentation and interpretation of the results highlighted a number of issues, including size and age, gender, exporting, and external knowledge. Small young firms tend to grow faster than larger, older firms do, especially for low-tech firms using firewood as their power source. Female firms are likely to have lower growth rates. Exporting has a positive effect on growth, especially for young firms and also female firms. Proprietary firms face lower growth on the whole, especially for young proprietary firms.

Although some small firms in our dataset are able to convert knowhow into commercial success, many others do not have any technical knowledge, and those who do are unable to use it profitably.

Finally, we explore the most pressing issues faced by different kinds of declining firms and obtain several interesting insights into the factors that act as barriers to the growth of small firms in a developing country context. The results for the barriers to firm growth models suggest that the main problems faced by female firms seem to concern raw materials, and market problems. Rural firms are vulnerable to problems concerning raw materials, equipment, management, and also power shortages, while they are relatively less exposed to problems concerning labour and lack of demand.

Appendix 1

Table 5.5 Variable definitions

Variable	Definition
Firm Growth (for the two-year period from financial year 1999–2000 until financial year 2001–02)	log (*Gross Output2001–2002*) – log(*Gross Output1999–2000*)
Size	log (*Gross Output1999–2000*)
Age2002	Log of age of the firm as of 2002 = log (2002-year of initial production)
ProprietaryOwnership	Proprietary owner firm.
Woman	The enterprise is owned and operated by a woman
Power source	This variable takes values: No power needed, Coal, Oil, Liquefied petroleum gas (LPG), Electricity, Non-Conventional energy, Traditional energy/Firewood
Technical knowledge	This variable takes values: No technical knowhow, technical knowhow obtained from abroad, and technical knowhow obtained from a domestic collaborating firm or R&D institution or specialized agency.
Industrial sector	Two Digit Industry Classification following India's National Industrial Classification of 1998 (NIC1998)
Urban	Urban = 1 if the firm is located in an urban region
Export	Export = 1 if the firm exports a positive share of its output

References

Acs, Z. J. (2006). How is entrepreneurship good for economic growth. *Innovations, 1*(1), 97–107.

Aftab, K., & Rahim, E. (1989). 'Barriers' to the growth of informal sector firms: A case study. *Journal of Development Studies, 25*(4), 490–507.

Aghion, P., Burgess, R., Redding, S., & Zilibotti, F. (2005). Entry liberalization and inequality in industrial performance. *Journal of the European Economic Association, 3*(2–3), 291–302.

Allen, F., Chakrabarti, R., De, S., Qian, J., & Qian, M. (2006). *Financing firms in India*. World Bank Policy Research Working Paper 3975.

Autio, E. (2008). *High- and low-aspiration entrepreneurship and economic growth in low-income economies*. Paper presented at the UNU-WIDER project workshop on Entrepreneurship and Economic Development, Helsinki.

Autio, E., Sapienza, H., & Almeida, J. (2000). Effects of age at entry, knowledge intensity, and imitability on international growth. *Academy of Management Journal, 43*(5), 909–924.

Balakrishnan, P., Parameswaran, M., Pushpangadan, K., & Babu, M. (2006). Liberalization, market power, and productivity growth in Indian industry. *Journal of Policy Reform, 9*(1), 55–73.

Banerjee, A., & Duflo, E. (2007). The economic lives of the poor. *Journal of Economic Perspectives, 21*(1), 141.

Barron, D. N., West, E., & Hannan, T. M. (1994). A time to growth and a time to die: Growth and mortality of credit unions in new york, 1914–1990. *American Journal of Sociology, 100*(2), 381–421.

Beck, T., Demirguc-Kunt, A., & Levine, R. (2005). SMEs, growth, and poverty: Cross-country evidence. *Journal of Economic Growth, 10*(3), 199–229.

Bigsten, A., Collier, P., Dercon, S., Fafchamps, M., Gauthier, B., Gunning, J., et al. (2004). Do African manufacturing firms learn from exporting? *Journal of Development Studies, 40*(3), 115–141.

Bigsten, A., & Gebreeyesus, M. (2007). The small, the young, and the productive: Determinants of manufacturing firm growth in Ethiopia. *Economic Development and Cultural Change, 55*(4), 813–840.

Blasnik, M. (1998). *LMS: Stata module to perform least median squares regression fit*. Boston College Department of Economics, Statistical Software Components number S358301.

Blau, D. M. (1985). Self-employment and self-selection in developing country labor markets. *Southern Economic Journal, 52*(2), 351–363.

Bottazzi, G., Coad, A., Jacoby, N., & Secchi, A. (2010). Corporate growth and industrial dynamics: Evidence from French manufacturing. *Applied Economics*, forthcoming. https://doi.org/10.1080/00036840802400454.

Clerides, S., Lauch, S., & Tybout, J. R. (1998). Is Learning by exporting important? Micro-dynamic evidence from Colombia, Mexico and Morocco. *Quarterly Journal of Economics, 63*, 903–947.

Coad, A. (2007). A closer look at serial growth rate correlation. *Review of Industrial Organization, 31*(1), 69–82.
Coad, A. (2009). *The growth of firms: A survey of theories and empirical evidence.* Cheltenham, UK: Edward Elgar.
Coad, A. (2010). Investigating the exponential age distribution of firms. *Economics: The Open-Access, Open-Assessment E-Journal, 4*(2010–17), 30.
Das, S. (1995). Size, age and firm growth in an infant industry: The computer hardware industry in India. *International Journal of Industrial Organization, 13*(1), 111–126.
Dunne, T., Roberts, M., & Samuelson, L. (1989). The growth and failure of US manufacturing plants. *Quarterly Journal of Economics, 104*(4), 671–698.
El-Namaki, M. S. S. (1988). Encouraging entrepreneurs in developing countries. *Long Range Planning, 21*(4), 98–106.
Evans, D. S. (1987a). The relationship between firm growth, size and age: Estimates for 100 manufacturing industries. *Journal of Industrial Economics, 35*, 567–581.
Evans, D. S. (1987b). Tests of alternative theories of firm growth. *Journal of Political Economy, 95*(4), 657–674.
Fizaine, F. (1968). Analyse statistique de la croissance des entreprises selon l'age et la taille. *Revue d'économie politique, 78*, 606–620.
Geroski, P. A., & Gugler, K. (2004). Corporate growth convergence in Europe. *Oxford Economic Papers, 56*, 597–620.
Giloni, A., Simonoff, J. S., & Sengupta, B. (2006). Robust weighted LAD regression. *Computational Statistics and Data Analysis, 50*, 3124–3140.
Grossman, G., & Helpman, E. (1991). *Innovation and growth in the world economy.* Cambridge, MA: MIT Press.
Günther, I., & Launov, A. (2006). Competitive and segmented informal labor markets. IZA Discussion Papers 2349, Institute for the Study of Labor (IZA) September
Fields, G. S. (2005). *A guide to multisector labor market models.* Social Protection Discussion Paper Series No. 0505, World Bank.
Harris, J. R., & Todaro, M. P. (1970). Migration, unemployment and development: A two sector analysis. *American Economic Review, 60*(1), 126–142.
Huergo, E., & Jaumandreu, J. (2004). How does probability of innovation change with firm age? *Small Business Economics, 22*(3), 193–207.
Hisrich, R. D., & Ozturk, S. A. (1999). Women entrepreneurs in a developing economy. *Journal of Management Development, 18*(2), 114–124.

Kochhar, K., Kumar, U., Rajan, R., Subramanian, A., & Tokatlidis, I. (2006). India's pattern of development: What happened, what follows? *Journal of Monetary Economics, 53*(5), 981–1019.

Krishna, P., & Mitra, D. (1998). Trade liberalization, market discipline and productivity growth: New evidence from India. *Journal of Development Economics, 56*(2), 447–462.

Leff, N. H. (1979). Entrepreneurship and economic development: The problem revisited. *Journal of Economic Literature, 17*, 46–64.

Little, I. M. D. (1987). Small manufacturing enterprises in developing countries. *World Bank Economic Review, 1*(2), 203–235.

Liu, J., Tsou, M., & Hammitt, J. (1999). Do small plants grow faster? evidence from the Taiwan electronics industry. *Economics Letters, 65*(1), 121–129.

Maloney, W. F. (2004). Informality Revisited. *World Development, 32*(7), 1159–1178.

McPherson, M. A. (1996). Growth of micro and small enterprises in Southern Africa. *Journal of Development Economics, 48*, 253–277.

Mead, D. C., & Liedholm, C. (1998). The dynamics of micro and small enterprises in developing countries. *World Development, 26*, 61–74.

MSME. (2009). Annual Report 2008–09, Ministry of Micro, Small and Medium Enterprises, Government of India, Retrieved May 21, 2010, from http://msme.gov.in

Phillips, B., & Kirchhoff, B. (1989). Formation, growth and survival; small firm dynamics in the US economy. *Small Business Economics, 1*(1), 65–74.

Reichstein, T., & Dahl, M. (2004). Are firm growth rates random? analysing patterns and dependencies. *International Review of Applied Economics, 18*(2), 225–246.

Robson, P., & Obeng, B. (2008). The barriers to growth in Ghana. *Small Business Economics, 30*(4), 385–403.

Rodrik, D., & Subramanian, A. (2005). From 'Hindu growth' to productivity surge: The mystery of the Indian growth transition. *IMF Staff Papers*, 52(2).

Rogerson, C. (1996). Urban poverty and the informal economy in South Africa's economic heartland. *Environment and Urbanization, 8*(1), 167.

Rousseeuw, P. J., & Leroy, A. (1987). *Robust regression and outlier detection* (Wiley series in probability and mathematical statistics). New York: John Wiley and Sons.

Shanmugam, K., & Bhaduri, S. (2002). Size, age and firm growth in the Indian manufacturing sector. *Applied Economics Letters, 9*(9), 607–613.

SIDBI. (2001). SIDBI Report on small scale industries sector, Small Industries Development Bank of India. Retrieved May 21, 2010, from http://dcmsme.gov.in/publications/traderep/sidbirep.pdf

Singh, S. P., Reynolds, R. G., & Muhammad, S. (2001). A gender-based performance analysis of micro and small enterprises in Java, Indonesia. *Journal of Small Business Management, 39*(2), 174–182.

Sleuwaegen, L., & Goedhuys, M. (2002). Growth of firms in developing countries, evidence from Côte d'Ivoire. *Journal of Development Economics, 68*(1), 117–135.

Stinchcombe, A. (1965). *Social structure and organizations* (pp. 142–193). Indianapolis, IN: Bobbs-Merrill.

Tamvada, J. P. (2010). Entrepreneurship and welfare. *Small Business Economics, 34*(1), 65–79.

Thorson, J. A. (1994). The use of least median of squares in the estimation of land value equations. *Journal of Real Estate Finance and Economics, 8*, 183–190.

Tybout, J. R. (2000). Manufacturing firms in developing countries: How well do they do, and why? *Journal of Economic Literature, 38*, 11–44.

Variyam, J. N., & Kraybill, D. S. (1992). Empirical evidence on determinants of firm growth. *Economics Letters, 38*, 31–36.

Wennekers, S., Van Stel, A., Thurik, R., & Reynolds, P. (2005). Nascent entrepreneurship and the level of economic development. *Small Business Economics, 24*(3), 293–309.

Western, B. (1995). Concepts and suggestions for Robust regression analysis. *American Journal of Political Science, 39*(3), 786–817.

Yasuda, T. (2005). Firm growth, size, age and behavior in Japanese manufacturing. *Small Business Economics, 24*(1), 1–15.

You, J.-I. (1995). Small firms in economic theory. *Cambridge Journal of Economics, 19*, 441–462.

6

Conclusion: The Dual Theory

This chapter analyses entrepreneurship in light of the previous chapters of this book, which provide insights into the nature of entrepreneurship in a developing country. At the outset, we link the occupational choice of individuals and entrant firms' start-up size in the spatial context that simultaneously determines the two processes. This link is established using a simple model of occupational choice, firm start-up size and the spatial location. Furthermore, we summarize the results on returns to entrepreneurship. Finally, we link the dynamics of entrepreneurship to the process of economic development.

6.1 The Dual Theory of Entrepreneurship

Chapter 2 shows that spatial location is an important micro-determinant of self-employment choice. Using geoadditive models and Bayesian semi-parametric techniques, the probability of self-employment choice is estimated here as a function of personal characteristics, educational background and spatial location.

J. P. Tamvada, *Microentrepreneurship in a Developing Country*,
https://doi.org/10.1007/978-3-030-68628-4_6

Using a database of about 90,000 people in India collected in 2004, the estimation shows simultaneous co-existence of neighbourhoods that induce people into self-employment, and neighbourhoods that decrease the probability of self-employment. One striking observation of the estimated spatial patterns of self-employment is that the likelihood of individuals to be self-employed is high in regions that are relatively poor. While this can be explained to some extent by the dual labour market hypothesis, that considers parallel existence of formal and informal submarkets in less developed countries due to job rationing, it also suggests that the returns to self-employment in a developing country are likely to be lower than returns to salaried employment as the propensity to be self-employed is higher in poorer regions.

In Chap. 3, the returns to entrepreneurship are estimated using a direct measure of welfare, the per-capita consumption expenditure of the household. The returns of being an employer, a self-employed worker, a salaried employee, or a casual labourer are estimated using quantile regressions. A hierarchy of welfare amongst individuals of different occupations is discovered that is persistent across quantiles. While households headed by employers have highest per-capita consumption expenditure, households headed by self-employed individuals are slightly poorer than those headed by salaried employees. Households headed by casual labourers are the poorest. This hierarchy is found to persist even after controlling for the industrial sectors to which the individuals belong. However, the quantile regression estimates for urban and rural regions show that while the difference between the self-employed and salaried employees increases in rural regions, it vanishes at three of the five quantiles in the urban regions.

Chapter 4 highlights that the start-up size is not independent of the geographic location. Once again, using geoadditive models, the effect of spatial location is estimated as a micro-determinant of the start-up size in this chapter. Using a database of 150,000 start-ups in the manufacturing sector, the analysis shows that the start-up size of firms is spatially skewed, with spatial effects crossing boundaries of the districts and states. The analysis suggests the presence of distinct spatial patterns of start-up size. It is further seen that financial and economic development positively predict start-up size in the region.

It is compelling to observe here that these geographic patterns of the start-up size of new firms are related to the spatial neighbourhood patterns of self-employment choice. Chapters 2 and 4 together give startling revelations about the nature of entrepreneurship across the space. It is seen that many regions that have higher likelihood of self-employment, as suggested by Chap. 2, are also the regions that have smaller start-up size. This, in essence, suggests that self-employment in the region is linked to start-up size. In particular, regions that give birth to firms of larger size are likely to absorb the labour force that would have been compelled to choose self-employment otherwise. This leads to a reduction in self-employment levels in more developed regions. In regions that are less developed, individuals are compelled to start firms of smaller size. A further analysis of these regional differences suggests that improving access to finance, amongst other factors, contributes to a larger start-up size. Thus, public policy should aim to accelerate financial development of regions that are lagging behind. Furthermore, a proactive policy to create large enterprises, even if they are state owned, can provide impetus to regions' microentrepreneurs, as such large-scale investments can lead to economic development that positively impacts the size of new start-up firms by providing them new opportunities through agglomeration economies.

Chapter 5 examines the factors shaping growth and decline of small firms in India. It suggests that enterprises managed by women have lower expected growth rates and proprietary firms face lower growth on the whole, especially if they are young firms. Exporting has a positive effect on firm growth, especially for female-owned firms and for young firms. Also, the results here suggest that while some small firms are able to convert knowhow into commercial success, many others are unable to translate it into superior growth. Thus, public policy can steer the accelerated growth of small firms by facilitating their exports and creating institutional support in the form of training to enable small firms to build and further capitalise on their knowledgebase.

We formalize some of these arguments in a simple model of occupational choice, firm start-up size and the geographic location. For simplifying the representation of the spatial context in the model, we define the *Entrepreneurial Climate* of a region as the constellation of region specific factors that determine entrepreneurship.[1]

[1] A region defined by its institutional factors that include its technical and research institutions, financial markets, and industrial structure is expected to influence both the rate of entry and its quality.

6.2 Formalizing the Findings

6.2.1 A Simple Model

The model builds on the model of regional entrepreneurship of Georgellis and Wall (2000), that can be summarized in the following two equations:

$$P\left[s_{rj}=1\right]=P\left[U_r^{se}-U_r^{pe}+\delta_r>0\right]$$
$$\Rightarrow S_r=\frac{1}{L_r}\sum_{j=1}^{L_r}P\left[s_{rj}=1\right]=F\left[U_r^{se}-U_r^{pe}+\delta_r\right] \qquad (6.1)$$

Here the probability of choosing self-employment in a region is modelled in terms of the difference between the utilities of choosing self-employment and paid employment. S_r is the proportion of people who opt for self-employment in region *r*, L_r is labour force of the region, s_{rj} refers to the individual *j* in region *r*, U_r^{se} is the utility of self-employment in the region *r*, and U_r^{pe} is the utility of paid employment. Thus, their model predicts the self-employment rate in a region as a function of the differences between both utilities and a random term that differentiates an average person in region *r* from the rest of the average person of the whole economy.

It is assumed that there is only one industry in which firms can enter. Furthermore, it is assumed that there are *n* regions that are similar in every manner except in their entrepreneurial climates. The model builds on the model of Georgellis and Wall (2000) by first considering $S_r \times L_r$ as a function of time and then defining net entry rate as a differential of $S_r \times L_r$ with respect to time. Let X_t^r be entrepreneurial climate in region *r* at time *t*, then:

$$S_r \times L_r = f\left(X_t^r\right) \qquad (6.2)$$

Considering e_t^r as the net entry rate in region *r* at time *t*, the net entry rate is given by

$$e_t^r=\frac{\partial f}{\partial t} \qquad (6.3)$$

In order to keep the model simple, there is no exit in the regions. This assumption implies that the above equation gives the number of entrants in a region at time *t*.

For notational simplification, assume that each x_k is such that $\frac{\partial e_t^r}{\partial x_k} > 0, x_k \in X$. Then X_t^r can be used to order regions on the strength of entrepreneurial climates, where $\|.\|$ is a simple distance metric.

Thus, $X_t^p > X_t^q$ implies that the entrepreneurial climate in region *p* is better than the entrepreneurial climate in region *q*. Let the initial start-up size of a firm *j* entering region *r* at time *t* be given by V_{jt}^r.

There are two types of entries. Let T be the threshold such that, if $V_{jt}^r < T$, the firm is found on very poor initial conditions.

Let the set of entrants in a region be E_t^r. This set can be partitioned in two subsets E_{1t}^r and E_{2t}^r based on the threshold condition $V_{jt}^r < T$. The first subset, E_{1t}^r, consists of firms that violate the threshold condition. Then, $e_{mt}^r = \left|E_{mt}^r\right|$ for $m = 1, 2$ (where |.| refers to the cardinality of the set) gives the number of entrants of each type at time *t*. A higher proportion of type 1 entrants increases the average start-up size of entrants.

This average start-up size of all entrants at time *t* in region *r* is given by,

$$\mu_t^r = \frac{1}{e_t^r} \int_{j \in E_t^r} V_{jt}^r \tag{6.4}$$

The papers in this thesis suggest that regions that have a poor entrepreneurial climate increase the probability of entry but entrants are very small in size. The following two propositions are derived based on the empirical analysis in the previous chapters.

The *proposition of cardinality*: Self-employment is likely to be higher in regions with poorer entrepreneurial climates ($X_t^p > X_t^q \Rightarrow e_t^p < e_t^q$).

The *proposition of initial conditions*: If entrepreneurial climate in a region *p* is better than the entrepreneurial climate in a region *q*, then the mean start-up size of entrants in region *p* should be higher than the mean start-up size of firms in region *q* ($X_t^p > X_t^q \Rightarrow \mu_t^p > \mu_t^q$).

These two propositions suggest that self-employment is inversely related to start-up size of new firms.[2] Also, if the labour force is stable, in region *p* people move out of self-employment into wage employment, while in region *q* people are compelled to become self-employed, as new firms do not absorb the excess labour force. Thus, regions with superior entrepreneurial climates give birth to superior entrants who absorb the excess labour force that would be self-employed otherwise. This leads to a reduction in self-employment over time. The empirical evidence presented in the book supports these propositions.

6.2.2 The Dual Curve

The dual curve in Fig. 6.1 captures the relationship between entrepreneurship and economic development. As results in Chap. 2 suggest, educated individuals are likely to move into salaried employment in nonagriculture. Given the findings in Chap. 3, this is plausible, as individuals get a signal about the relative welfare afforded by different occupations, a hierarchy in which self-employment comes lower than salaried employment. Furthermore, a superior entrepreneurial climate resulting from the process of development induces entrepreneurs to enter with a higher firm size (Chap. 4). Thus, while in the beginning there is high level of subsistence driven self-employment, the level drops with economic development. This is shown by the curve of subsistence entrepreneurship (SE). Simultaneously, a different type of entrepreneurship emerges in the form of employers, self-employed professionals and micro-entrepreneurs who start-up with larger firm-sizes. These gradually increase in number in regions that have superior entrepreneurial climates that are driven by economic, financial development, and large-scale industrialization, amongst other factors. This is shown by the curve of scalable growth orientated entrepreneurship (GE). The curve TE shows the aggregate entrepreneurship and the curves SE and GE are components of TE. Thus,

---

[2] Under certain assumptions, it can be analytically shown that entry of type 1 (where the threshold condition is not satisfied and the start-up size is higher than T), $e1t^{p}$, will be higher than e_{1t}^{q}, suggesting that regions with better entrepreneurial climates induce better firms to enter. Conversely, it can also be shown that $e2t^{p}$ would be lower than e_{2t}^{q}.

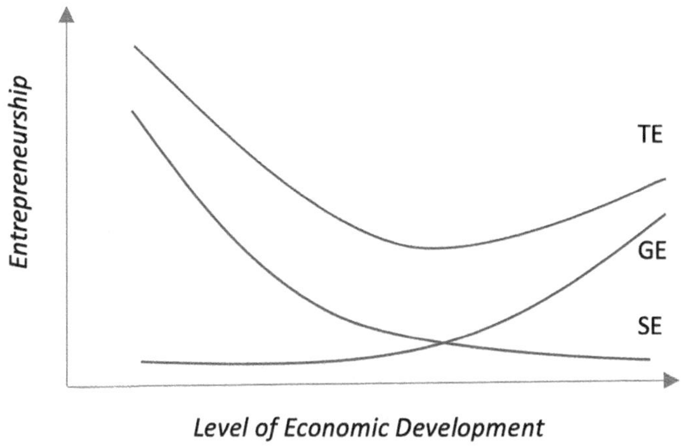

Fig. 6.1 Entrepreneurship and economic development

entrepreneurship in a developing country assumes a variety of forms, and a policy focus on one form of it may not do justice to the entire spectrum of entrepreneurial activity.

6.3 Conclusions and Policy Implications

This chapter builds a coherent theory linking self-employment choice with the start-up size of new firms and the spatial location. In particular, it argues that self-employment should not be viewed independently of the firm size of entrants in a region. Higher levels of self-employment are mostly correlated inversely with the size of entrants. A high level of entrepreneurship, given by a high degree of entrepreneurial activity in a region, should go hand-in-hand with a larger initial size of new firms for entrepreneurship to make an impact on the economy. The chapter also defines the entrepreneurial climate for linking self-employment of individuals and the start-up size of firms in a region using a simple theoretical model and suggests that superior entrepreneurial climates lead to better entrants in the region. Such entrants are likely to absorb the excess labour force leading to a reduction in the level of people who may be compelled to opt for self-employment otherwise.

Educated individuals will aspire to move into salaried employment with economic development, although they may come back to entrepreneurship as growth-orientated entrepreneurs in later stages of development. In line with the knowledge spillover theory of entrepreneurship (Acs et al., 2009), such growth-orientated entrepreneurs are likely to tap into unexploited opportunities that arise when new knowledge gets created. Thus, it is essential to promote cutting-edge research while developing the capabilities of individuals to exploit such knowledge spillovers by investing in higher education infrastructure and increasing access to it.

Public policy should facilitate the occupational transitions from casual labour into self-employment as it entails higher economic returns. Similarly, economic processes that accelerate economic and financial development, such as those that increase financial accessibility, are prerequisites for the emergence of growth-orientated start-ups. Investments in infrastructure development and large-scale industrialisation can provide exploitable opportunities along the vertical chain to new entrepreneurs. Such investments can create a solid foundation for the emergence of an entrepreneurial economy. In the absence of these, policies that solely focus on creating more start-ups can result in new firms that are sub-optimal in size and concentrated in sectors with low minimum efficient scale or technology-intensive sectors that are accessible to select individuals. For existing small firms, policy interventions that facilitate access to working capital, learning and exports, and offer additional support to women-led businesses can address the barriers to their growth. For these reasons, developing countries should not undermine their focus on improving the overall ecosystem that can lead to more impactful start-ups and accelerated growth of existing enterprises.

References

Acs, Z. J., Audretsch, D. B., Pontus, B., & Carlsson, B. (2009). The knowledge spillover theory of entrepreneurship. *Small Business Economics, 32*(1), 15–30.

Georgellis, Y., & Wall, H. J. (2000). What makes a region more entrepreneurial? Evidence from Britain. *Annals of Regional Science, 34*, 385–403.

Index[1]

[1] Note: Page numbers followed by 'n' refer to notes.

J. P. Tamvada, *Microentrepreneurship in a Developing Country*,
https://doi.org/10.1007/978-3-030-68628-4

Printed by Printforce, the Netherlands